Supper for a Song

Supper
for a Song

Tamasin Day-Lewis

RIZZOLI
NEW YORK

New York · Paris · London · Milan

Photography by JAMES MERRELL

How to cook a chicken . . . again and again — 6

The Saturday bake — 34

Pot luck: single-pot dinners — 54

Happy food — 72

Use your loaf — 92

Supper for a song — 122

The fruit glut — 152

Something-out-of-nothing suppers — 164

Index — 186

Notes • Use fresh herbs, coarse salt, and freshly ground black pepper unless otherwise suggested. • Use large eggs, organic or at least free-range. Anyone who is pregnant or in a vulnerable health group should avoid recipes that use raw egg whites or lightly cooked eggs. • Timings are for conventional ovens. If using a convection oven, reduce the temperature by 25 degrees F. Use an oven thermometer to check the temperature.

How to cook a chicken...

This is not meant to be an insult; after all, you all know how to cook a chicken, but maybe you're not so good at making the bird pay full fare.

You've had your Sunday dinner, cleared up the greasy roasting pans, and filched the final potato. The last thing you feel like doing is getting the stockpot going. You put the bare bones, carefully wrapped, in the fridge for tomorrow, or the next day, or next week—when you'll find them there staring at you accusingly and chuck them away. But you somehow can't quite bring yourself to throw them away now.

Or you've given everyone giant second helpings, not wanting to be stingy, not wanting to say you would really like to keep a leg and a breast aside for supper the next day. You will have to start cooking from scratch again tomorrow. It will cost time and money, which is infuriating when you could have been halfway there—needing only to raid the fridge and your imagination to come up with Chicken Reincarnation.

I'm sure you have all wished you had been just a little more think-aheaded about things. And that having thought ahead, you would be all set to spice up those errant wings you clipped before the bird got trussed and roasted, and slow-cook them in a brew of lime and ginger, garlic and molasses, chili and more chili, and dunk them into a blue cheese dressing.

If only you hadn't stripped the meat from your roast as close as a GI haircut down to the carcass and ripped every last scrap from

again and again

its undercarriage until there wasn't a pick of flesh left on it. If you had stretched the bird as far as it would go, there would be a heap of extra stuffing, thick with onion and sage, to deliver to your table on a dull, dreary Monday night in the shape of a magnificent savory pie with a golden crust. All for so much less effort than if you'd had to start from scratch. And you would still have stock for a soup and other juicy morsels to plop into a creamy lemon chicken risotto, where the meat is not really center stage—it is a walk-on part.

When I'm creating something out of nothing, or turning the old into new, I really feel I am cooking. You could say it is hard-times cookery, "willful waste makes woeful want," and all that, but it is so satisfying that ultimately it is less about the scrimping and saving and putting a secondhand rose on the plate than it is about showing you are a creative cook and can work with whatever you've got on hand.

What do we throw away most? Chicken carcasses, lettuce leaves and limp vegetables, scraps of cheese and stale bread, chickpeas that we've cooked too many of, and old, cold potatoes. The list is as long as your shopping list.

There is a wonderful expression that says when you eat a pig you should eat everything but the squeal. That is what this chapter is about, and here are some ways you can do it and feel proud of yourself, proud that you used up every last little bit and what you made was a supper that made you sing.

Roast chicken
with sausage, sage, and prune stuffing

The point of buying a larger-than-you-need chicken is that you can give it an encore. Roast a generously stuffed, good-sized chicken and serve it with lots of different vegetables, including potatoes and parsnips, and you really don't need to offer large helpings of meat. There will be plenty left over to make a risotto, pot pie, or salad. You can also double the amount of stuffing to yield enough to make a sausage pie for supper the following evening (page 13). If you do not have sage, prunes work well with thyme, too.

Serves 6 (in its first incarnation).

1 organic or at least free-range chicken, about 4½ to 5½ pounds (giblets saved for gravy)

1 large onion, peeled and sliced

a little olive oil

coarse salt and black pepper

for the stuffing

1 pound good pork sausages

2 tablespoons olive oil

a walnut-size knob of butter

1 red onion, peeled and minced

2 celery stalks, strings removed with a potato peeler and finely chopped with a few leaves

about 12 sage leaves, minced

about 18 prunes, pitted and roughly chopped

2 slices stale bread, crusts removed and blended in a food processor to crumbs

finely grated zest of 2 organic oranges

1 organic large egg, beaten

for the gravy

¾ cup red wine

vegetable cooking water (ideally from potatoes and parsnips)

Preheat the oven to 400 degrees F. Have the chicken ready at room temperature. Put the sliced onion in the bottom of your roasting pan.

For the stuffing, slit the sausage skins and drop the meat into a large bowl; set aside. Heat the olive oil and butter in a heavy-bottomed skillet and add the onion, celery, and minced sage. Cook over medium-low heat until the vegetables have begun to soften and turn translucent. Throw in the prunes and remove from the heat a couple of minutes later; do not stir them around too much, as you don't want them to turn mushy. Let cool slightly, then add to the sausage meat with the bread crumbs and orange zest. Season lightly, as the sausages will be seasoned already. Now add the beaten egg and gently turn the mixture until it coheres.

Stuff the chicken and secure the opening. Set the bird on the sliced onion in the roasting pan, douse with a little olive oil, season with salt and pepper, and put into the oven to roast. A bird this size should take between 1 hour 20 minutes and 1 hour 40 minutes, by which time the skin will have crisped and turned bronze. Add the giblets to the roasting pan for the last 20 minutes. To test if it is cooked, insert a skewer into the thickest part of the thigh. If the juices run clear, not bloody, the bird is cooked.

Transfer the chicken to a warm platter and leave to rest, covered loosely with foil, in a warm place for 10 to 15 minutes while you make the gravy, and finish the accompanying vegetables before carving. For the gravy, pour off any excess fat from the roasting pan, then set it over medium-high heat. Add the wine and stir with a wooden spoon to deglaze, crushing the chicken liver as you do so. Let bubble for a minute or two, then add the cooking water and let bubble to reduce and thicken to the desired consistency. Press through a sieve into a warm gravy boat or pitcher.

Slice the breast thinly and give everyone a few slices and either a wing or a piece of leg, depending on appetite and how much meat you would like left over. Give everyone a generous helping of stuffing. Pour all the juices from the carving board into the gravy. Remove the bird from sight!

Cover the remains of the bird once it has cooled, but do not pick the meat at this stage unless you are going to make stock immediately, as it dries much more quickly off the carcass.

Spicy chicken wings
with blue cheese dressing

I am convinced it's a male conspiracy that girls are supposed to like the light meat and boys the dark, as the best-flavored meat on a chicken is the dark. After all, what the men carve for themselves must be the best. And there are so many people who don't make the best use of every little nook and cranny of their chick. Why do we cut the feet off? The French don't, nor do the Chinese; they know that ten toes add a lovely glueyness to stocks and soups in the same way as the addition of a pig's trotter does.

At the Taunton, Somerset, farmers' market on a Thursday, Jason, of The Ark Chicken Company, is only too pleased that a few of us are not demanding only chicken breasts. He sells wings by the bag, and they are the most delectable of things to get your tongue around and suck and pick right down to the bone. Add a spicy sauce, and you have an appetizer that doesn't look amiss at a good dinner—the cost bearing no relation to the sumptuousness of the taste.

Start this recipe the night before so the bones have time to marinate.

Serves 4 as an appetizer.

12 to 16 chicken wings

for the marinade

2 teaspoons toasted sesame oil

1 heaping tablespoon blackstrap molasses

1 heaping tablespoon golden syrup

2 tablespoons ketchup

juice of 1 lime

piece of fresh ginger, approx. 1" square, peeled and grated

2 garlic cloves, peeled and crushed

1 red chile, seeded and finely minced, or 1 dried chile, crumbled, or 1 teaspoon chile flakes, or cayenne pepper to taste

for the dressing

3 tablespoons sour cream

6 tablespoons homemade mayonnaise

2 teaspoons Worcestershire sauce

¼ teaspoon crushed garlic

coarse salt and black pepper

3 ounces blue cheese, such as Stilton or Roquefort, crumbled

Mix all the marinade ingredients together and taste—you may want to adjust the quantities depending on your spiciness and sharpness. Throw the chicken wings into a large Ziploc bag and pour in the marinade. Seal the bag, squelch it around a bit, and leave to marinate overnight in the fridge.

For the blue cheese dressing, whisk the sour cream, mayonnaise, Worcestershire sauce, and garlic together in a bowl with some seasoning, remembering that the cheese will be quite salty. Fold in the crumbled cheese, check the seasoning, cover, and chill until you need it.

Bring the chicken wings to room temperature before you cook them. Preheat the oven to 275 degrees F. Line a baking dish, large enough to hold all the wings in a single layer, with foil. Place the wings on the tray and pour over the marinade. Cook for about 2 hours, turning them over from time to time to make sure the sauce doesn't dry out.

Serve the chicken wings hot on a platter with the chilled blue cheese dressing, so that everyone can help themselves and dip the wings into the dressing.

Lemon chicken risotto

A little chicken goes a long way in this dish, which is an adaptation of a recipe by my favorite Italian food writer, Anna Del Conte. It has the soothing quality a proper risotto should have, with its almost chalky-textured rice, which combines bite and firmness with sloppiness.

I normally use the king of risotto rice, carnaroli, for this dish, but Arborio or vialone nano might suit your budget better.

Serves 4.

1 tablespoon olive oil

2 tablespoons unsalted butter

2 shallots, peeled and finely minced

1 celery stalk, strings removed with a potato peeler and finely chopped

1⅓ cups risotto rice

4 cups vegetable or chicken stock

6 sage leaves, rolled up and shredded

1 small sprig of rosemary, needles chopped

finely grated zest and juice of 1 organic lemon

1 organic large egg yolk

4 tablespoons freshly grated Parmesan, plus extra to serve

4 tablespoons heavy cream

coarse salt and black pepper

¾ cup cooked dark and white chicken meat, diced

Heat the olive oil with half of the butter in a heavy-bottomed medium saucepan and add the shallots and celery. Cook gently, stirring occasionally, for about 7 minutes until softened (this is a *soffritto*). Add the risotto rice and stir to coat for a couple of minutes.

Heat the stock and keep it at simmering point throughout the cooking. Pour about ½ cup onto the rice and stir vigorously until most of it has been absorbed, then add some more and stir again until absorbed. Continue in this way, adding the chopped mixed herbs and lemon zest roughly halfway through cooking, which takes about 20 to 22 minutes altogether.

In a small bowl, combine the egg yolk, half of the lemon juice, the Parmesan, and the cream, then add a generous amount of black pepper. Mix well with a fork.

When the rice is cooked but still *al dente*, take the pan from the heat and stir in the egg and cream mixture, cooked chicken, and remaining butter. Add another ladleful of hot stock.

Cover the pan and leave to rest for 5 minutes off the heat. Check the seasoning and adjust if necessary, adding more lemon juice if you think it is needed. Give the pan a short stir and serve at once, with extra Parmesan passed around in a bowl.

You can omit the cooked chicken from the recipe if you like and just serve the risotto on its own with a green salad to follow. Or for a traditional Milanese dish, sauté some chicken pieces in butter to color, then cook them in a casserole in the oven with 1 cup of heavy cream, and serve the lemon risotto as an accompaniment.

Sausage pie

This is real food, outdoors food fit for an early fall picnic or a cold day's walk. Good sausage meat, spicing, and pie crust, it is comforting stuff, made a little lighter and more elegant by having no top deck and only the best ingredients. Fine, too, for a bracing walk along the beach.

If you are making the stuffing especially for the pie, you may prefer to omit the fruit from the stuffing and just go porky. It's up to you.

Serves 6.

for the pie crust

1¼ cups (scant) all-purpose flour

pinch of coarse salt

6 tablespoons (¾ stick) chilled butter, cut into cubes

1 to 2 tablespoons cold water

for the filling

1 recipe sausage stuffing (page 9, or use the alternative below)

Preheat the oven to 375 degrees F. Sift the flour and salt into the food processor, add the butter cubes, and pulse until the mixture resembles crumbs. Add 1 tablespoon water through the feed tube and process briefly until the dough forms a ball, adding more of the water if necessary. Wrap in plastic wrap and put it into the fridge to rest for 30 minutes.

Roll out the pie crust on a lightly floured surface to a large circle and use to line a 9" flan pan. Line the pastry case with a piece of waxed paper and a layer of dried beans and bake "blind" for 15 minutes. Remove the paper and beans, then prick the pie crust with a fork and return to the oven for 5 minutes.

Pile the stuffing mixture quickly and gently into the pie crust shell, smoothing it down with a spatula. Bake for about 30 minutes until the top is browned and the filling is cooked; it should not have dried out.

Leave the pie to stand for 10 to 15 minutes before serving. It goes very well with homemade tomato sauce (page 174) or just a dab of English mustard. If serving cold, cool completely on a wire rack.

Pork and apple stuffing

This is a great alternative for a sausage pie or to stuff a roast chicken, or you could make double to yield enough for both. Peel, core, and slice 2 tart eating apples, such as McIntoshes. Finely chop 1 onion, 1 garlic clove, and 2 thumb-size pieces of ginger. Heat 2 tablespoons olive oil and a knob of butter in a large skillet and gently fry the onion, garlic, and ginger with the apples and a handful of torn sage leaves until the onion has softened. Take off the heat, let cool a little, then tear in a crustless, thick slice of bread. Add 1 pound sausage meat and a beaten egg, mix well, and season judiciously.

Poaching a chicken and saucing it up

You may decide to stretch your chicken in a different direction and poach it to begin with, rather than roasting it. This is a lovely mild and gentle thing to do with a good bird, and you can still use any leftover meat for the lemon chicken risotto (page 11) in the same way.

A simple cream sauce thickened with egg yolk and sharpened with lemon is wonderful with a poached bird and carries on the ivory-colored theme. You may serve the vegetables you have poached it with, too, and when the bird is stripped and done, plop the carcass back in the poaching liquid with a fresh set of vegetables to turn it into stock. Once strained, this doubly intense stock makes a lovely base for a soup—chicken or otherwise.

My absolute favorite way with a poached chicken is the dish opposite, chicken Savoyarde. Poaching also gives you the best-textured meat for a chicken pie, in my case with a layer of buttery leeks and a béchamel made with half chicken stock, half milk, and lots of celery, onion, parsley, and mushrooms. That way less meat is needed, yet the pie is big on flavor.

Chicken stock

If you are using the carcass from a roasted chicken for your stock, it is worth roasting the bones to intensify the flavor, keeping the fat and skin on the bird for an even better taste. That is if you can be bothered. Sometimes I do, sometimes I don't. The bones from a poached chicken are not worth browning, as they aren't dry enough.

Don't worry if you don't have all the suggested vegetables for your stock; just use more of the ones you do have. If you haven't used the chicken giblets for gravy, throw them in the pot, too.

Place your stockpot over lively heat, hurl in the bones and broken-up carcass, and brown on all sides for a few minutes; or do this in the roasting pan in a hot oven, instead, if you'd rather, then transfer them to the pot.

Add a large onion, skin on for flavor and color, halved and spiked with 2 cloves; a fat leek, cleaned and cut in half; a large carrot in chunks; 2 celery stalks with a few leaves, broken into shorter lengths; a bouquet of parsley, thyme, rosemary, and bay; and enough water to cover. Bring to a boil, skim off any scum from the surface, and turn down to a low simmer, putting the lid on. Cook at a gentle burble for 2 hours.

Leave the stock to cool in the pot, then strain it into a large bowl, cover, and refrigerate. When the fat has solidified, skim it off. Now your stock is ready to use.

Chicken Savoyarde

This is a dish for a special occasion, and the quality of the ingredients is paramount. It is the first thing I cook when the autumn chill descends on us and we want a hearty dinner that boasts creamy richness, but is still one step short of the ballast one needs in winter. It has given more pleasure to more people than any other dish I can think of, and to me, the cook, too. Loyal followers who have come across it before, please spare a thought for new readers. It is my classic favorite. All you'll need to accompany it is steamed broccoli and some potato and celeriac puree. Something green is important, for color on the plate.

Don't be put off by the amount of tarragon, an herb that is inclined to overwhelm with the taste of aniseed. Here, mellowed by the Gruyère, cream, and white wine, it finds its own strength and subtlety to perfection, without stealing the show.

Serves 6 (with some to spare).

to poach the chicken

1 organic or at least free-range chicken, about 4½ to 5½ pounds

2 onions, peeled and each stuck with a clove

2 large carrots, peeled and cut into chunks

3 celery stalks, cut into chunks

green tops of 2 or 3 leeks, well washed

a small bunch of herbs (thyme, rosemary, parsley, and 2 bay leaves), tied together

6 peppercorns

for the sauce

4 tablespoons (½ stick) butter

⅓ cup (generous) all-purpose flour

1¾ cups reserved poaching stock (from the chicken)

1¼ cups dry white wine, warmed

1 cup heavy cream, warmed

¾ cup (rounded) grated Gruyère

1 tablespoon Dijon mustard

1½ cups chopped tarragon leaves

coarse salt and black pepper

for the topping

1 cup bread crumbs

¼ cup freshly grated Parmesan

To poach the chicken, put the bird into a heavy-bottomed pot in which it fits cozily and surround with the vegetables, herbs, and peppercorns. Just cover with cold water. Bring to a boil, skim off any scum from the surface, and turn the heat down to a low simmer. Cover and poach gently for about 1¼ to 1½ hours. The water must be at a bare shudder.

Either cool the bird in its poaching liquid or, if you are serving the dish immediately, remove it to a board and strain the stock into a bowl, discarding all the solids. Leave it to settle, then remove the surface fat.

Strip all the meat from the chicken if you are using it all for the dish; if not, remove enough for 6. Discard the skin and tear the meat with the grain into long, thinnish strips. Preheat the oven to 425 degrees F.

To make the sauce, melt the butter in a pan, stir in the flour, and let it bubble for a couple of minutes until it turns a light tan. Gradually add the hot poaching stock, a ladleful at a time, alternately with the wine and cream, whisking to keep the mixture smooth. When all of the liquid has been added and the sauce has been cooking for around 20 minutes so it has no residual floury taste, add the Gruyère, mustard, tarragon, and salt and pepper.

Continue to cook the sauce over a low heat for about 15 to 20 minutes. Taste and adjust the seasoning and mustard if you need to, then consider the balance of cheese, cream, and wine, which should each have its place without being predominant.

Put the chicken into an au gratin dish and pour the sauce over the bird. Sprinkle with bread crumbs and then with Parmesan. Bake for 20 to 25 minutes until the top is golden brown and bubbling with little eruptions of sauce bursting through. Wait 10 minutes before serving.

Ground meat

As always, it is all about quality, not quantity. Lesser ground meat—invariably watery and more fatty than anything you will buy from a good butcher—cannot be transformed into a great dish by sprucing it up with spices, vegetables, or anything else, for that matter. Far better to buy good-quality ground meat and use it more sparingly. The organic longhorn beef I buy by the quarter-steer from a local farmer works out no more expensive than endless trips to the supermarket shelves for vastly inferior meat.

My ragout sauce has onion, carrot, celery, garlic, and enough tomato—at least 2 cups to a pound of meat—to flavor and color the final sauce, after three hours' simmering, with the richest and deepest of tones. That way, what might serve two or three people if you were focusing on meat, feeds six. They won't complain for lack of meat when they've got the powerful alchemy of slow-cooked good ingredients to contend with on the plate, and all the flavors have married into an oily rich, intensely flavored dish that bears no resemblance to, well, ground meat.

Even if you don't have a meat grinder—and I don't—you can do the next best thing with the remains of your leg or shoulder of lamb and chop it as small as small can be. I always buy shoulder, not just because it is more economical, but because I love the more intense, fattier flavor.

Obviously cooked ground meat is a different beast to deal with from the raw stuff, but only in terms of its cooking time and texture, which will never be quite so absorbent or malleable as starting from fresh. Just think of it as a different dish.

Shepherd's pie, cottage pie

In Britain, this is the classic Monday night supper after a Sunday roast if you've cooked a roast of lamb or beef larger than you need, which I invariably do. Depending on how much meat you have left, adjust the amount of vegetables and potatoes accordingly. And keep back some dark gravy, rich with meat juices, so that you can intensify the flavor of the meat without stock.

In the fall or winter, a cottage (beef) or shepherd's (lamb) pie made with half parsnip and half mashed potatoes is a lovely variation—grate some sharp Cheddar over too, if you like. And do try my alternative cottage pie (illustrated).

Serves 4.

1½ pounds or thereabouts cooked beef or lamb, left over from a roast

3 tablespoons olive oil

1 large onion, peeled and minced

2 celery stalks, strings removed with a potato peeler and minced

2 medium carrots, peeled and finely diced

3 garlic cloves, peeled and chopped

2 tablespoons tomato paste

a few shakes of Worcestershire sauce

a few drops of Tabasco

2 or 3 anchovies, minced (optional)

¼ to ¾ cup or thereabouts gravy, left over from the roast

½ cup red wine

2 pounds floury potatoes or half potato, half parsnip or celery root

4 tablespoons (½ stick) butter or more, plus extra for dotting on top

½ to ¾ cup hot milk, or more

coarse salt and black pepper

nutmeg for grating

2 tablespoons coarsely grated sharp Cheddar (optional)

Grind the meat or chop it very small by hand. Heat the olive oil in a large, heavy-bottomed skillet and throw in the onion, celery, carrots, and garlic. Stir over medium heat until they begin to soften and turn translucent, about 7 minutes.

Add the meat and stir to brown evenly, over livelier heat. After about 5 minutes, add the tomato paste, Worcestershire sauce, and Tabasco to heat things up a little. Add the anchovies, if using, mashing them in with a fork—they will bring out the flavor of the meat without making it taste at all fishy.

Stir the gravy into the meat mixture and then add the red wine. Simmer gently for about an hour to bring all the flavors together.

About 20 minutes before the end of the cooking time, preheat the oven to 400 degrees F. Boil the potatoes and any roots separately in the usual way until tender. If using potatoes only, drain and mash with the butter and hot milk. If using parsnip or celery root with the potatoes, you will not need milk, just mash them together with butter and a little of the roots' cooking water. Season the mashed mixture, adding a little nutmeg, too.

Put the meat into a baking dish, cover with the mashed potatoes, and scatter the grated cheese over the potatoes, if using. Dot the top with little flecks of butter. Bake for 30 to 40 minutes or until browned in patches and bubbling. Serve with frozen peas and tomato ketchup.

Alternative cottage pie

I made this discovery one evening when I was short of potatoes and lacking a few other ingredients. It was the best cottage pie ever.

Omit the carrots if you don't have any, but include the anchovies. Use 2 tablespoons tamari sauce in place of the Worcestershire sauce for a lovely depth and complexity of flavor. If you haven't any wine open, add a splash of Marsala or Madeira instead. Add a 14-ounce can of tomatoes and simmer everything together for 2½ hours, as you would for a ragout.

For the topping, use one-third celery root to two-thirds potato and stir through 2 sautéed sliced leeks (the green part and the white).

Italian meat loaf

If you think this sounds too big for you or your family, don't worry; not only does it freeze well, but it also is portable picnic food and works brilliantly in a sandwich with some English mustard or mango chutney. Eke it out.

Inspect your fridge for this dish, as really it's the odds and ends of cheese, ham or bacon, tomatoes, and eggs that you can change around, deciding on what stratum you are going to run like a seam through the meat. Green olives are great with ground pork or veal, a few capers tucked in are good with the parsley, and so is a little anchovy with the egg. Fontina makes a good alternative to Gruyère or Comté.

Serves 8 to 10.

1 pound ground beef or veal

1 pound ground pork

4 organic large eggs, beaten

2 large garlic cloves, peeled and minced

1 large onion, peeled and finely minced

2 tablespoons chopped flat-leaf parsley

1 teaspoon chopped thyme, or you can use tarragon or sage

coarse salt and black pepper

3 or 4 plum tomatoes, skinned, seeded, and sliced

3 organic large eggs, boiled for 6 minutes, cooled, shelled, and sliced

7 ounces cooked bacon or pancetta, or prosciutto or ham

18 or so large green olives, pitted and chopped (optional)

1 tablespoon capers, rinsed, drained, and chopped (optional)

6 anchovies, drained and minced (optional)

1 ounce each Parmesan and either Gruyère or Comté, grated (about 1 tablespoon)

Preheat the oven to 300 degrees F. Oil a terrine or loaf pan, about 12 x 4" and 4" deep.

Put all the meat into a large mixing bowl with the beaten eggs, garlic, onion, and herbs. Season generously and mix well with your fingers. Pack half the mixture into the prepared mold.

Layer the tomato slices over the meat mixture, then add the sliced boiled eggs. Chop or finely slice the bacon or ham and arrange on top. Combine whatever optional pantry items you are using and scatter over the meat, then sprinkle with the grated cheeses.

Pack the rest of the meat mixture down firmly on top and lay a sheet of greased parchment paper on the surface. Put the lid on, or cover tightly with foil if you are using an open loaf pan. Boil a kettleful of water.

Stand the terrine or loaf pan in a roasting pan and pour in enough hot water to come halfway up the sides of the mold. Cook on the middle shelf of the oven for 1 hour. Uncover and bake for another 15 to 30 minutes until browned on top and cooked right through. Insert a skewer into the center of the loaf to check that it is cooked.

Serve hot, with tomato sauce and buttered boiled or baked potatoes, or cool in the pan and serve cold.

If you have any leftover ground meat mixture, roll it into small walnut-size balls, pushing a knob of mozzarella into the center of each. Lightly roll in flour and fry, turning, until evenly colored and cooked through, adding some tomato sauce (page 174) for the last 5 minutes of the cooking time to heat through with the meatballs. Serve with pasta and pass around grated Parmesan.

Too much mashed potatoes

You can never have too much mashed potato. I defy you to. I can eat epic quantities of it when it is made with floury potatoes, rich whole milk, and lovely French or Italian butter, stirred in with coarse salt and a good scrunch of black pepper. My personal best was after running a marathon—the great white mountain on the plate disappeared in record time, too. It felt like a couple of pounds, but that day, for once, I knew I'd earned my excess.

For my mashed potatoes, I put the hot potatoes through the coarse disk of a food mill straight back into the pan in which they were boiled, having melted the butter and heated the milk in the pan while the potatoes are in the food mill. I do it over a gentle heat and stir everything together with a wooden spoon.

Colcannon and champ, those simple, special Irish ways with spuds, really cannot be bettered. Scallions softened in hot milk for champ, and cooked cabbage and leeks for colcannon (page 57). For total indulgence, pour a stream of melted butter into a crater on the summit of the mashed mixture for you to stir in with your fork.

There are so many simple, yet wondrous, things to do with mashed potatoes the second time around, it is worth making far, far too much, so that there is no danger of eating it all at the first sitting, and every danger of having the base for tomorrow's breakfast, lunch, or supper sitting there ready for you.

Think of a crisply fried potato cake, or potato and celeriac cake, of crêpes Parmentier, the most delectable of potato pancakes, which will hold anything from blood sausage to smoked eel, from crisp bacon to chicken livers. Or frizzle a little leftover cabbage in butter with whole-grain mustard and you've got a "bubble and squeak" to drape a few bacon strips over or serve with a sausage.

If you are using leftover mashed potatoes, don't keep them in the fridge overnight, for something awful happens to them, flavor-wise. Instead, keep them covered in a cool pantry or similar. Here are some of the things I love turning old, cold mashed potatoes into, such good things that nobody would even guess at their being yesterday's remains.

Potato bread

For this recipe you need only a mound of leftover mashed potatoes to make the most delectable breakfast treat: potato bread or potato farls. It is a real Irish comforter, to smother with melting butter and scrunch a little pepper over. Or serve the warm triangles with a few slices of crisply fried blood sausage or eggs, bacon strips, or a sausage, to make you remember how breakfast ought to be.

My Northern Irish neighbor Patricia rushed through the door one bitterly cold morning with a little foil package of warm, buttered farls for a late-morning snack. I tucked into one and felt better immediately. This is her recipe.

Serves 3 (or 2 greedies).

1 cup mashed potatoes
⅓ cup all-purpose flour
pinch of coarse salt
extra flour for dusting
butter and black pepper
to serve

Push the mashed potatoes through a potato ricer, or sieve into a bowl, and sift in the flour. Season with salt and mix thoroughly. Bring together with your hands to make a ball.

Dust your worktop with flour and roll out the dough to roughly an 8" circle. Cut out 6 triangular wedges, as you would a cake.

Put a cast-iron or other heavy-bottomed skillet over moderate heat for a few minutes to heat up. Dust lightly with flour and put the farls snugly in the pan. Cook for about 10 minutes until golden brown; they won't brown evenly. Turn over and repeat.

Remove to a wire rack and allow to cool slightly for a minute, then rub on butter until it melts and grind some pepper over. Eat right away.

Eva's potato apple cake

The same neighbor, Patricia, of the aforementioned potato bread, says this cake would have been cooked in poor households all over Ireland during the early 1900s on a griddle over an open fire. It was very much a "high days and holidays" treat, and Patricia's mother, Eva, made it frequently. Sadly, she has now passed away, so it has become Eva's potato apple cake.

The idea that leftover mashed potatoes were considered a luxury, along with a few cooking apples and sugar, may be a thought somewhat alien to our times, but it is how I like to see food—be it the simplest, most poorly perceived ingredients. It reminds me of a trip I made to Puglia, in Italy, region of la cucina povera ("the poor kitchen," peasant food), based almost entirely on vegetables and bitter weeds, and tostata (the chaff left behind from harvesting), which is toasted and turned into pasta the color of wild mushrooms. It is as exciting a cucina as any I have sampled and as full of simple, unusual, inexpensive treats as this Irish counterpart, made of apples and potatoes.

Serves 4.

2 cups mashed potatoes
¾ cup (rounded) all-purpose flour, plus extra to dust
pinch of coarse salt

for the filling
2 large cooking apples
¼ cup (scant) unrefined superfine vanilla sugar

Push the mashed potatoes through a potato ricer, or sieve into a bowl, and sift in the flour. Add the salt and mix thoroughly. Bring together with your hands to make a ball.

Divide the dough in half and roll out one half into an 8" circle, placing it on a lightly floured plate. On a floured surface, roll out the second ball to a circle just a little larger than the first.

For the filling, peel, quarter, core, and finely slice the apples into a bowl. Scatter the sugar over, turning the apple slices to coat them.

Pile the apple mixture on top of the dough circle on the plate, leaving a border free around the edge. Using a pastry brush, dampen the edge with a little water. Put the other dough circle on top and press the edges firmly together to seal.

Heat a shallow heavy-bottomed or cast-iron pan over moderate heat for a few minutes. Scatter a little flour over the surface. Carefully slide the potato cake into the pan and cook for 15 to 20 minutes until golden underneath.

Slide the cake out of the pan and back onto the plate, then invert onto another, lightly floured plate. Slide the cake back into the pan to cook the other side for 15 to 20 minutes.

Carefully transfer to a warmed serving plate and serve in wedges with whipped cream.

Parmesan potato cake
with mozzarella and prosciutto

I have adapted this beautiful dish from
a recipe of the great Anna Del Conte.
You may start with freshly made mashed
potatoes if you like, but it really is as good
to use yesterday's. You just need to think
ahead and add the butter, milk, nutmeg,
Parmesan, and eggs when you originally
mash the potatoes so that everything melts
in properly.

It is a warming lunch or supper dish, which
works well served with some slow-cooked
gratinéed tomatoes and a green salad.
Ashamed of the idea of serving a souped-up
potato cake for a supper party? You won't
be with this dish, particularly if you use
really good ingredients, such as a proper
aged Parmigiano-Reggiano and a good
prosciutto such as San Daniele.

Serves 4.

scant 2 pounds floury potatoes, peeled and cut into large chunks

⅓ cup hot whole milk

6 tablespoons (¾ stick) butter

coarse salt and black pepper

pinch of freshly grated nutmeg

6 tablespoons freshly grated Parmesan

3 organic large eggs, plus an extra yolk, beaten

14 ounces mozzarella di bufala, sliced

3 ounces prosciutto (about 6 slices)

3 ounces mortadella or salami (a salami with fennel seeds works well)

1 tablespoon chopped flat-leaf parsley (optional)

for the base and top

4 to 5 tablespoons stale bread crumbs (brown or white)

1½ tablespoons butter

Preheat the oven to 400 degrees F. Boil the potatoes in the usual way until they are cooked through, then drain and mash well, adding the hot milk and butter. Season and add the nutmeg and Parmesan. Mix well, then add the beaten eggs and extra yolk and mix again. Set aside.

Butter an 8" springform cake pan and scatter about a third of the bread crumbs over it. Spoon half the potato mixture over. Cover with the sliced mozzarella, prosciutto, mortadella or salami, and parsley, if using.

Spoon the rest of the potato mixture over this, then sprinkle with the rest of the bread crumbs and dot with butter.

Bake for about 30 minutes until the potato cake is browned and crisp on top and bubbling in the middle. Let it stand on a wire rack for 10 minutes before unhinging the side of the pan and removing it.

Cut the potato cake into thick wedges like a cake. Serve with a simple Belgian endive salad, dressed with a vinaigrette, and slow-cooked tomatoes on the side.

Chick-peas

Always soak more than you need. Lovely leguminous things work as well on the side as they do mainstream; it's just a question of thinking them through. If you soak and cook a package of dried chickpeas, you can turn a third into creamy hummus and make soups, salads, and stews with the rest, or even stuff bell peppers with chickpeas and Indian-style spices.

If you love falafel (page 33), you may wish to soak half of your chickpeas for somewhat longer, as these tasty morsels are made from the raw peas, which require a full 24 hours' soaking.

Here's what to do with the humble beady chickpea.

Hummus and chickpeas to spare

I don't understand the false economy of supermarket hummus—I've simply never tasted one that didn't remind me of wallpaper paste. Soaking legumes is not, after all, hard work. Unless you've got a crowd to feed, just use a third of the chickpeas for the hummus and refrigerate the rest in their gelled cooking liquid for up to three days to use for other dishes.

to cook the chickpeas

1 cup (generous) dried chickpeas, soaked in cold water for at least 8 hours

1 onion, spiked with a clove

handful of leek tops, a celery stalk, and a carrot (or any of these)

6 peppercorns

2 bay leaves

for the hummus

1 to 2 lemons

1 to 2 tablespoons tahini paste (the toasted sesame paste is ideal)

2 or 3 garlic cloves, peeled and chopped

4 to 5 tablespoons olive oil

coarse salt and black pepper

1 teaspoon cumin seeds, toasted and crushed (optional)

splash of good extra-virgin olive oil

a small handful of cilantro leaves, chopped (optional)

Drain the chickpeas and place in a heavy-bottomed pot. Add enough water to cover by about ¾", but don't add salt at this stage. Add the flavoring vegetables, peppercorns, and bay leaves. Bring to a boil, lower the heat, and cover. Simmer until tender, 1½ to 2 hours, depending on the age of the chickpeas.

To make the hummus, put one-third of the chickpeas into a blender with 2 to 3 tablespoons of the cooking liquid. Add the juice of 1 lemon, 1 tablespoon tahini, 2 garlic cloves, 3 to 4 tablespoons olive oil, some seasoning, and the cumin if you are using it. Blend to a puree.

Now taste critically. You will probably need the juice of at least another half a lemon, some more salt, and possibly a little more tahini, though there should be just a hint, not a hit, of this. Assess the garlic too; it shouldn't overwhelm but you should know it's there. You may want to loosen the puree with a little more cooking liquid and a little more olive oil. It depends on your palate—how you like it best.

When you are happy with your hummus, scrape it into a small terrine or bowl and mark with the top of a knife to give a ridged surface. Now swirl a little peppery green olive oil over the surface.

Either cover and refrigerate for a few days and use as needed or serve at once, with grilled pita bread or raw crunchy vegetables. A little freshly chopped cilantro strewn over the top of the hummus before you serve it will alleviate the desert color.

Chorizo and chickpea stew
with piquillo peppers

Oh the bliss of a quick supper where the initial cooking has been done and you need only fry an onion and do a little simmering. The smoky, the piquant, the controlled heat, and the earthiness of the individual components transform this dish into a hearty, tasty peasant Spanish stew. Eat it straight from the bowl, no extras needed; it's just as good the following day.

Serves 6.

1 cup dried chickpeas, soaked in cold water for at least 8 hours

3 cups vegetable or chicken stock

1¼ cups crushed tomatoes

2 tablespoons olive oil

2 medium onions, peeled and minced

1¼ pounds good-quality chunky chorizo sausage, cut into bite-size chunks

3 or 4 garlic cloves, peeled and minced

8-ounce jar wood-roasted piquillo peppers, or use skinned, roasted fresh red bell peppers

1 teaspoon smoked paprika

coarse salt and black pepper

a handful of flat-leaf parsley, chopped

Cook the chickpeas in the stock and tomatoes in advance until tender, about 1½ to 2 hours.

Heat the olive oil in a heavy-bottomed pan and gently fry the onions until softened. Throw in the chorizo and fry, turning the chunks as you go, for about 10 minutes. When the chorizo starts to release its characteristic red, oily fat, add the garlic, then the chickpeas along with their liquid.

Cut the peppers into long, thin strips and add them to the pan with the smoked paprika. Simmer gently for another 10 minutes, then taste and season. Ladle into bowls and sprinkle some parsley over.

If you can't find crushed tomatoes, put the same quantity of canned whole tomatoes through a food mill.

Chickpea and smoked paprika soup

This is something to make in a hurry with your leftover chickpeas when you want a hearty, simple soup and don't have any time or any stock. Don't overdo the smoked paprika—it should exude a slightly smoky mystery to the soup, not the obvious taste of full-blown paprika.

Serves 4.

1 tablespoon olive oil

1 red onion, peeled and minced

3 garlic cloves, peeled and minced

2 celery stalks, strings removed with a potato peeler and chopped small

2 teaspoons finely chopped rosemary needles

2 cups cooked chickpeas

¼ to ½ teaspoon smoked paprika

2 bay leaves

1 level tablespoon tomato paste

14-ounce can diced tomatoes

4 to 5 cups water, or use stock if you have it

coarse salt and black pepper

a small handful of flat-leaf parsley, chopped

Heat the olive oil in a large, heavy-bottomed pot and add the onion, garlic, celery, and rosemary. Sauté for a few minutes until they begin to soften, then add the chickpeas, smoked paprika, bay leaves, tomato paste, and canned tomatoes. Bring to a simmer, then add the water, season, and bring back to a boil. Lower the heat and simmer for 10 minutes.

Discard the bay leaves. Process about half the mixture in a blender, then reintroduce it to the chunky soup in the pot. Taste and adjust the seasoning, stir in the parsley, and reheat if you need to. Ladle into warm bowls and serve.

Falafel with tahini cream sauce

These little fried spiced chickpea balls are great served with drinks or as a picnic snack. They are especially good dipped into the tahini cream sauce, but you can simply serve them with yogurt flavored with a crushed garlic clove, 1 teaspoon ground toasted cumin, and some seasoning, if you prefer.

Because the chickpeas are used raw, you need to remember to put them to soak a full 24 hours ahead.

Makes about 24.

4½ cups dried chickpeas, soaked in cold water for 24 hours

1 large onion, peeled and minced

3 garlic cloves, peeled and minced

2 green chiles, seeded and minced

1 red chile, seeded and minced

a handful of flat-leaf parsley, chopped

a handful of cilantro leaves, chopped

2 teaspoons cumin seeds

2 teaspoons coriander seeds

coarse salt and black pepper

2½ cups peanut or grapeseed oil, for shallow-frying

tahini cream sauce

2 garlic cloves, peeled

juice of 2½ or 3 lemons

½ cup tahini paste

2 tablespoons live-culture goat's, sheep's, or cow's milk yogurt

2 to 3 tablespoons cold water

1 teaspoon toasted cumin seeds, ground

a handful of flat-leaf parsley, chopped

Drain the chickpeas and dry them on a clean dish towel. Put them into the food processor with the onion, garlic, chiles, and chopped herbs. Grind the cumin and coriander seeds in a mortar, then add to the processor with some seasoning. Blend the mixture to a grainy-textured pulp; the chickpeas will give it this texture. Transfer to a bowl.

Take walnut-sized pieces of the mixture and form into little patties. You can either cook them immediately or keep them covered in the fridge until needed; they will be fine to cook the next day.

To make the tahini cream sauce, crush the garlic with a little salt. Put it into a bowl with 1 tablespoon of the lemon juice and stir. Add the tahini and stir it in, followed by the rest of the lemon juice and the yogurt. Add enough water, a spoonful at a time, to make a thick, smooth cream. Add the cumin and taste. The flavor needs to be tart and strong, so add a touch more garlic, lemon juice, salt, or spice as needed.

When ready to eat, spoon the sauce into a bowl and sprinkle with the parsley. Heat the oil for shallow-frying in a heavy-bottomed pan. Drop a crumb of the falafel mix in to check that it is hot enough; it will resurface instantly and bubble away if it is. Fry the patties in small batches for about 4 minutes until deep golden brown, turning after a couple of minutes. Drain on a warm plate lined with paper towels.

Serve the hot, crisp falafel with the tahini cream sauce and warm pita bread, if you like.

> **The tahini cream is a lovely sauce, by the way, to serve alongside a conventional roast shoulder or leg of lamb.**

The Saturday bake

In this new age of packed-lunch fever, when we are growing more pumpkins than petunias for the first time ever, when we're reading seed packets, not cornflake boxes, sowing herbs in window boxes, mulching tomatoes on roof terraces, and saving our energy, there is no food that changes and nourishes our lives, our souls, more than baking.

Baking is the food of memory. Even if our mothers didn't stand us on the kitchen chair to sift flour, roll dough, and primp jam tarts, it is a memory we all wish to have, imagine having. When we are children, when we are students, it is the form of cooking that most makes us grow in cooking confidence, and it is the food that we like to eat. During childhood, our hearth and our hearts are in the kitchen; then, when we leave home, baking is the food that most reminds us of it. And it is the food we can afford as students. What price a stack of cookies, a sticky cake, a brownie, a warm, buttered tea loaf? We can bake with an almost empty pocket. We may not always feel like making the effort, but when we do, we wonder why we don't more often.

When my friend Georgie talks about her childhood, she always goes back to the "Saturday bake." Money may have been scarce, but there was always a sense of plenty. Georgie's mother did all the baking for the week ahead with all four children. They made cornflake cakes, cupcakes, butterfly cakes with wings, sticky ginger cake, and shortbread dotted with cherries, currants, or apple. At Sunday teatime there were sandwiches and cakes— always a fruit cake for Georgie's dad, which then went into the children's lunch boxes every day—and usually a Victoria sponge cake spilling raspberry jam and cream. "I never remember my mother buying a cake or a cookie," Georgie tells me.

When my three children were tiny, my kitchen was really not very different. The smallest baby, Charissa, would be in her baby bouncer dangling from a kitchen ceiling hook, or in the playpen, Miranda and Harry up to no good somewhere in the garden or— once the scent of baking wafted past their nostrils—clambering to taste and decorate whatever I was making. Earliest toy? A wooden spoon.

Saturday afternoons were an immovable feast and still pretty much are: a favorite jazz record request program blaring from the radio, the KitchenAid swirling, the Cuisinart whirring, the weekend's cakes, brownies, and cookies hitting the stove, then the cooling rack. Wicked fingers will be trying to snitch a corner here, a crumb there, before the steam has fully escaped and a warm, damp cinnamon-tinged carrot cake is cool enough to cut.

Baking is the first cooking we do as children, and with our own children, and it really doesn't matter if they begin by only wanting to lick the bowl and the spoon. A willing snacker turns into a willing cook pretty quickly, and it is the only way to learn without feeling it's a lesson. Nobody is scared of making pie crust if they don't know to be scared, nor do people fear a sponge cake not rising or a brownie not turning molten tender and gooey if they take part in the process young and the family has a kitchen that's always available to bake in. So have your own bake-in and reacquaint yourselves, if you need to, with one of the great joys of life: the Saturday bake.

Carrot cake
with lime and mascarpone topping

I have always loved a good, cinnamon-scented carrot cake but somehow found the normal cream cheese frosting too rich and too sweet for the cake. Carrots, after all, are sweet enough in their own right. However, this mascarpone topping—sharp textured with lemon and lime zest—contrasts perfectly with the texture and crunch of the carrots and walnuts. Take the path of least—if not no—resistance.

Makes an 8" cake.

1¼ cups all-purpose flour

2 level teaspoons baking powder

1 teaspoon ground cinnamon, preferably freshly ground

½ teaspoon ground cloves

½ teaspoon freshly grated nutmeg

1 cup light muscovado or light brown sugar

⅔ cup (scant) sunflower oil

2 organic large eggs

2½ cups coarsely grated organic carrots

¾ cup shelled walnuts, roughly chopped

for the frosting

1 lime

1 cup (scant) mascarpone

6 tablespoons (¾ stick) unsalted butter, softened

¾ cup unrefined confectioners' sugar

juice of ½ lemon, or to taste

Preheat the oven to 350 degrees F. Grease and line two 8" cake pans (or one deep pan). Sift the flour and baking powder together into a large bowl and mix in the spices.

Using an electric mixer, whisk together the muscovado (or brown) sugar, sunflower oil, and eggs until smooth. With a large metal spoon, fold in the grated carrots and chopped walnuts, then fold in the flour and spices until evenly combined.

Spoon the mixture into the prepared cake pan(s), set on a baking tray, and bake until a skewer inserted into the center comes out clean; test after 25 minutes for layer cake; 40 minutes for a deep cake. Leave to cool in the pan(s) on a wire rack.

For the frosting, pare a few shreds of lime zest with a zester and set aside; grate the rest of the zest and squeeze the juice from one half. In a bowl, beat the mascarpone with the softened butter, sugar, grated lime zest, and the lime and lemon juices. Taste. I like a good sharp topping, so sometimes add more lime, sometimes more lemon juice.

Sandwich the layers together with some of the mascarpone mixture, (or cut a deep cake into two layers). Spread the frosting over the top of the cake and smooth it down the sides to cover completely, then ruffle the surface. Either refrigerate or serve immediately, topped with the reserved zest. I like it a little cold, so that the frosting has set slightly.

Add snowdrops in season!

Chocolate cake

"Not another chocolate cake!" Those are the words I am least likely to utter. The deadline for this manuscript is tonight. What do I do? I can't write a book without a new chocolate cake recipe in it. So I make one. Perhaps this will be the best chocolate cake I've ever made. Who knows?

I make it anyway, on a whim. I've had an idea for a lighter-than-normal cake with a hint of coffee and crème de cassis, Marcona almonds, virtually no flour, and lots of bitter chocolate. Charissa is stricken with mumps and can't swallow. That leaves me and Georgie. I'll invite Patricia down the road, and Pete the postman is bound to deliver! Oh yes, it's fabulous, everyone agrees, light as a soufflé—and it takes only minutes to get it ready for the oven.

Makes an 8" cake.

²⁄₃ cup (scant) blanched Marcona almonds

5½ ounces dark chocolate, about 72% cocoa solids (I use Green & Black's "with added cocoa butter for easier melting")

1½ tablespoons crème de cassis

2 tablespoons strong espresso coffee

6 tablespoons (¾ stick) unsalted butter, cut into cubes

³⁄₈ cup (rounded) unrefined superfine vanilla sugar

3 organic large eggs, separated

1 level tablespoon all-purpose flour (optional)

Preheat the oven to 335 degrees F and heat a baking sheet. Butter an 8" springform cake pan generously. Grind the almonds in a blender or food processor until not quite finely ground.

Break up the chocolate and put it into the top of a double boiler (or a heatproof bowl), along with the cassis and coffee. Melt over hot but not simmering water, making sure the upper pan (or bowl) is not touching the water.

Add the butter, sugar, and ground almonds and take the pan off the heat, keeping the upper pan (or bowl) in place over the hot water. Stir the mixture until it is amalgamated. Beat the egg yolks and stir them in until combined.

In a clean bowl, stiffly whisk the egg whites. Scrape the chocolate mixture into a large bowl and stir in a spoonful of egg white. If adding the flour, sift it over the mixture and fold in. (Including the flour gives a slightly more coherent texture.) Fold in the rest of the whisked egg whites, a large spoonful at a time, as quickly and lightly as you can.

Spoon the mixture into the prepared pan and place on the preheated baking sheet on the middle shelf of the oven. Bake for about 50 minutes, but start testing the cake with a skewer after 40 minutes unless the middle is still obviously runny.

Leave to cool in the pan for 15 minutes, then release the sides of the pan and leave the cake to cool a little until it is just warm.

Eat immediately, with or without whipped cream. It will make your day. It is light and intense with a whiff of cassis and coffee. The edge has a slight crust, the middle is damp, like a mousse.

Dried apricot upside-down cake

Dark, burned-sugar stickiness, and sharp, unsulfured apricots make this cake a dessert favorite. Substitute fresh apricots in season; otherwise this is a perfect pantry recipe. You've probably got the ingredients already sitting there.

Makes an 8" cake.

for the topping

1 cup (scant) raw or turbinado sugar

½ cup water

4 tablespoons (½ stick) unsalted butter, cut into cubes

1¼ cups unsulfured dried apricots

for the cake

1½ cups all-purpose flour

2 slightly rounded teaspoons baking powder

4 organic medium eggs

¾ cup (rounded) unrefined vanilla sugar

8 tablespoons (1 stick) unsalted butter, melted and cooled to tepid

Preheat the oven to 335 degrees F. Grease an 8" springform cake pan.

To make the topping, dissolve the raw sugar in the water in a heavy-bottomed pan over medium heat, stirring. Turn up the heat so that the sugar syrup bubbles, and continue to cook until it is a dark mahogany color and looks syrupy when you swirl it around the pan.

Remove the pan from the heat and carefully add the butter cubes; the mixture will fizzle and pop. Pour it directly onto the base of the prepared pan and quickly tilt and turn the pan to coat the base and a little way up the sides; it will set quickly. Arrange the apricots firmly in the burned sugar base, in concentric circles.

For the cake, sift the flour and baking powder together. Whisk the eggs and sugar together using an electric mixer at full speed for about 10 minutes or until light, creamy, thick, and tripled in volume. Add the sifted flour and fold in gently and lightly, using a spatula. Finally fold in the melted butter.

Spoon the cake mixture evenly over the apricots in the pan. Bake for 50 minutes or until a skewer inserted into the center comes out clean.

Leave the cake in the pan on a wire rack to cool for 30 minutes or until the cake has shrunk away from the sides of the pan enough for you to release it. Invert the cake onto a large plate. Eat warm with whipped cream, or cold.

Almond cake with apricot jam

Home-ground Marcona almonds and a hint of bitter almond extract make this moist cake truly delectable. I have made it with a sharp hit of apricot jam, the kind that is good enough for the fruit to have kept shape and sharpness, and with Morello cherry jam, another of my favorites. Both work magic with almonds, it's up to you to choose. Serve the cake with afternoon tea or coffee, or serve it for dessert, perhaps embellished with some stewed fruit—plums, rhubarb, apricots, or figs.

Makes an 8" cake.

2 cups (rounded) blanched Marcona almonds

1 scant cup (2 scant sticks) butter, softened

1 cup (scant) unrefined superfine vanilla sugar

grated zest of 1 organic lemon

1 teaspoon natural almond extract

3 organic large eggs

$7/8$ cup (scant) all-purpose flour

1 heaping teaspoon baking powder

for the topping

3 heaping tablespoons best apricot (or Morello cherry or raspberry) jam

2 teaspoons water

Preheat the oven to 335 degrees F. Butter and flour an 8" springform cake pan. Grind the almonds in a blender or food processor until not quite finely ground.

Cream the butter and sugar together thoroughly using an electric mixer until pale and fluffy. Fold in the ground almonds by hand, along with the lemon zest and almond extract. Now beat in the eggs, one at a time. Sift the flour and baking powder together over the mixture and fold in gently with a metal spoon.

Spoon the mixture into the prepared pan and bake on the middle shelf of the oven for about 55 minutes until a skewer inserted into the center comes out clean; check after 50 minutes. Leave in the pan on a wire rack to cool, then turn out onto a plate.

Melt the jam with the water in a small pan over low heat and stir until just warm. Pour over the top of the cake and spread it around; it doesn't matter if it drips down the sides.

This cake keeps well since it is so damp with almonds. Serve it with or without whipped cream.

Vanilla sugar

For a constant supply, save vanilla beans once you have used them—either whole to infuse custards, etc., or after scraping out the seeds. Rinse and dry, then add to a large jar of sugar to impart fragrance and flavor. Keep adding beans to the jar as you use them—I have at least a dozen in mine!

Earl Grey fruit tea loaf

I first made this really fruity tea loaf with Fortnum and Mason's (of London) mixed dried fruits, which features dried strawberries, cranberries, and cherries, in addition to the more everyday golden raisins. It may be out of reach geographically and financially, but it certainly makes an everyday tea loaf special. I suggest you choose whatever combination of dried fruit appeals to you, but I will say that the mix of intensely sweet strawberry with sharp cherry and cranberry is one to aim for.

Consider blueberries, sour cherries, unsulfured apricots, and Muscat raisins—just a little more exciting than currants and raisins. And the leaf tea is as important, its bergamot, or smokiness, being absorbed by the fruit; choose Earl Grey or Lapsang leaves—the best quality you can find. A miniature of whiskey glugged into the mix before leaving it overnight can only add to the general pleasure.

This tea loaf keeps beautifully—wrapped in waxed paper and foil, or in a sealed tin, for up to a week. It also freezes well, so you might like to double the recipe and make two. Slice and butter, or toast for breakfast.

Remember to start the recipe a day ahead, as the fruit needs to steep overnight in the tea.

Makes one medium-size loaf.

2½ cups mixed dried fruit, such as Muscat raisins, unsulfured apricots, strawberries, cranberries, or cherries

⅝ cup (rounded) dark muscovado or dark brown sugar

1¼ cups Earl Grey or Lapsang tea, freshly made using 2 heaping teaspoons loose-leaf tea leaves

1⅜ cups self-rising flour

1 organic large egg, beaten

Put the dried fruit and sugar into a large bowl. Once the tea has brewed for 3 minutes, pour it over the fruit. Turn a few times before you go to bed, just to keep all the fruit lubricated. Leave overnight, until well plumped.

The next morning, preheat the oven to 350 degrees F. Grease and line a loaf pan, approx. 9 x 5 x 3". Sift the flour over the fruit in the bowl and add the beaten egg, then fold everything together.

Spoon the mixture into the prepared pan and bake for 1 hour, then turn the oven down to 310 degrees F and bake for another 25 minutes or until a skewer inserted into the center comes out clean.

Cool in the pan on a wire rack, then turn out. Wrap in foil or keep in an airtight container.

Chocolate brownies

No chapter on baking could eschew the brownie. I will try any good brownie recipe sent my way. After all, we are all seekers of perfection in chocolate heaven and need to believe we are just that much away from it each time. That way we have to try again.

When you test for doneness, you need a crumb but not a raw-looking crumb on the skewer—and a skewer pushed into the center, not the edge of the cake, please, as the outsides are always crumblier and less gooey.

Makes 12 to 16.

7 ounces dark chocolate, 64 to 74% cocoa solids

4 tablespoons strong, freshly made coffee, or 2 espressos, cooled until tepid

7½ tablespoons (scant 1 stick) unsalted butter, softened

1 cup (scant) unrefined superfine sugar

2 organic large eggs, plus an extra yolk

1 cup all-purpose flour

1 rounded teaspoon baking powder

a handful of blanched whole hazelnuts (optional)

Preheat the oven to 350 degrees F. Line the bottom and sides of a baking pan, 13 x 9" or thereabouts, with buttered foil.

Break up the chocolate and melt in a double boiler or in a heatproof bowl over a pan of hot water on low heat, making sure the bowl is not touching the water. Take off the heat and stir in the coffee.

Cream the softened butter and sugar together thoroughly, using an electric mixer, until light and fluffy. Beat in the eggs, one at a time, then add the egg yolk. With the mixer still running, add the chocolate and coffee mixture, amalgamate, and then turn off the machine.

Sift the flour and baking powder over the mixture and fold in, using a large metal spoon. Scrape the mixture into the prepared pan and level it with a rubber spatula. Push the whole hazelnuts, if using, into the mixture at intervals, so they just stand proud of it. Bake for about 25 minutes, then test with a skewer, as described above.

When the brownies are ready, place the pan on a wire rack and leave to cool. Cut into squares in the pan before removing.

You may like to serve the brownies with whipped cream or a scoop of vanilla ice cream.

Banana blondies

It's as though, baking-wise, the blonde never got a look-in. How often are you offered a "blondie" rather than a brownie—let alone a banana blondie? Scarcity value aside, blondies are irresistible, every bit as gorgeous as their dusky counterparts and so good with homemade vanilla ice cream. Adults only they are not; you will charm the children out of the trees or away from the screen with promises of either.

These banana babes are adapted from a recipe by Australian-born baking legend Dan Lepard, so their pedigree is top-notch.

Makes 16.

1¼ cups (rounded) unrefined superfine vanilla sugar

2 tablespoons water

⅔ cup (rounded) roughly chopped Brazil nuts

6½ tablespoons (generous ¾ stick) unsalted butter

7 ounces good white chocolate (I use Valrhona or Green & Black's)

2 bananas (roughly ½ pound)

1 organic large egg, beaten

1 vanilla bean, split, seeds scraped out

1⅓ cups (rounded) all-purpose flour

¼ teaspoon baking powder

Preheat the oven to 375 degrees F. Line the bottom and sides of an 8" square baking pan with foil.

Put ¼ cup (rounded) of the sugar into a small pan with the water. Dissolve over medium-low heat, then bring to a boil and let bubble until the sugar turns deep mahogany. To test, take a little of the syrup with a teaspoon and drop it into a glass of cold water; it should set to a hard ball.

Remove the pan from the heat and stir in the Brazil nuts, then immediately spread the toffee mixture onto an oiled baking sheet. Leave to cool, then chop the toffee finely.

Melt the butter and white chocolate in a double boiler or heatproof bowl over a pan of hot water, making sure the upper pan or bowl is not touching the water. Take off the heat.

Mash the bananas in another bowl and mix in the rest of the sugar, the egg, and the vanilla seeds. Add the melted chocolate mixture and stir until smooth. Sift the flour and baking powder over the mixture, then fold in, together with the chopped nutty toffee.

Scrape the mixture into the prepared pan and level it with a rubber spatula. Bake for about 35 minutes until golden on top, with a faintly wobbly set. Test with a skewer; it should come out with a crumb, not a raw bit of the mixture, attached. Place the pan on a wire rack and leave to cool. Don't slice until cold.

Serve the blondies with crème fraîche to sharpen them up, or with vanilla ice cream for total indulgence.

Whole-wheat date scones

These are slightly heavier than plain scones, but sweet and nutty at the same time and are great spread warm with butter for a proper breakfast. My neighbor Patricia brought around a little basket of them wrapped in a gingham napkin the morning the Oscars were announced in March 2008. I had been up since dawn watching the news of my brother Daniel's triumph as Best Actor for his role in There Will Be Blood. *All it needed was some Champagne and (blood!) orange juice and coffee to accompany the fruity scones.*

Makes about 10.

⅞ cup (scant) all-purpose flour

¾ cup whole-wheat flour

4 tablespoons (½ stick) unsalted butter, cubed and softened

1 tablespoon baking powder

½ teaspoon coarse salt

1 tablespoon brown sugar

⅔ cup roughly chopped pitted Medjool or other dates

⅝ cup whole milk

Preheat the oven to 425 degrees F. Sift the flours into a large bowl and tip in any bran left in the sieve at the end. Add the butter cubes and rub together with your fingertips as quickly as possible until you have a bread crumb consistency.

Stir in the baking powder, salt, and sugar, then throw in the dates. Make a well in the center and add the milk, mixing all together with a spatula to a soft dough.

Working quickly, turn the dough out onto a floured surface and very gently roll it out to a 1" thickness. Stamp out rounds with a 2" cookie cutter or the rim of an overturned small tumbler and place on a greased baking sheet. Bake for 10 to 12 minutes, or until well risen and golden. Cool on a wire rack.

These scones are best eaten warm with good salted or unsalted butter, according to your taste and mood.

Dried cranberry and cinnamon friands

These delightful little frivolities are perfect with coffee or tea, or you might serve a pile of them with ice cream and a bowl of mixed berries. You may prefer to make friands with fresh raspberries, blackberries, or blueberries, but here you have a sharp hit of dried fruit from something sitting waiting in your pantry.

Makes 10 to 12.

¾ scant cup (1½ scant sticks) unsalted butter

2¼ cups unrefined confectioners' sugar, plus extra to dust

⅝ cup (scant) all-purpose flour

1 cup ground almonds, preferably freshly ground Marcona almonds

1 tablespoon grated lemon zest (from about 2 organic lemons)

1 teaspoon ground cinnamon

2 organic large egg whites

⅔ cup dried cranberries

Preheat the oven to 400 degrees F. Grease 12 muffin cups. Melt the butter gently in a pan and cook until it is golden, not brown. Remove from the heat.

Sift the confectioners' sugar and flour into a large bowl. Add the ground almonds, lemon zest, and cinnamon and mix together, then stir in the egg whites. Pour in the melted butter and stir to combine.

Spoon the mixture into the greased muffin cups and scatter the cranberries over the mixture. Bake for about 15 minutes until light and springy to the touch, then leave to cool on a wire rack.

To serve, sift a little extra confectioners' sugar over the friands. The unrefined tastes so much better and more toffee-ish than the bright white kind.

Bay, honey, and lemon cake

There is something about fragrant, glossy-leaved fresh bay—a pure infusion of hope and aromatics. We often flavor meats with it, but tend to forget its talent and natural affinity with fruit. Bay is lovely macerated in a citrus syrup for a winter fruit salad (page 116) and in this unusual cake, with the lemon-syruped leaves wreathing the top like laurel with the thinly sliced lemons.

I like the taste and texture of whole-wheat flour in this cake, and its consistency when damp with the lemony syrup, but the choice is yours. If you are feeling particularly indulgent, you can spread homemade lemon curd between the two layers and arrive at an even richer heaven.

Makes a deep 8" cake.

1¾ cups Marcona almonds

1½ scant cups (3 scant sticks) softened butter

1 cup (scant) light muscovado or light brown sugar

¾ cup unrefined superfine vanilla sugar

4 organic large eggs

grated zest of 3 organic lemons (save the juice)

2⅛ cups whole-wheat or 2⅜ cups all-purpose flour, or 2¼ cups of each (mixed)

2 teaspoons baking powder

pinch of coarse salt

2 heaping tablespoons live-culture cow's, sheep's, or goat's milk yogurt

for the drizzle

2 heaping tablespoons strong-tasting clear honey, such as chestnut or acacia

1 organic lemon, thinly sliced, plus the juice of 3 lemons (see above)

8 to 10 fresh bay leaves

¼ cup (rounded) raw or turbinado sugar or ¼ cup unrefined granulated sugar

2 tablespoons water

for the filling (optional)

about 5 tablespoons homemade lemon curd

Preheat the oven to 350 degrees F. Butter two 8" springform cake pans and line the bottoms with waxed paper. Grind the almonds in a blender or food processor until not quite finely ground, to retain some texture.

Cream the softened butter and sugars together using an electric mixer until light and fluffy. Beat in the eggs, one at a time, then incorporate the lemon zest.

Sift the flour(s), baking powder, and salt over the mixture, adding any bran left in the sieve, and add the ground almonds. Fold in with a metal spoon until evenly combined. Stir in the yogurt, 1 tablespoon at a time, to give a soft dropping consistency.

Divide the mixture between the prepared cake pans. Bake on the middle shelf of the oven for about 40 to 50 minutes until a skewer inserted into the center comes out clean.

While the cake is baking, prepare the drizzle. Put the honey, lemon juice, bay leaves, sugar, and water into a heavy-bottomed pan and stir over low heat until the sugar has dissolved. Bring to a boil and let bubble hard for 10 minutes or until you have a sticky syrup when you swirl it around the pan. Now add the sliced lemon, without seeds. Let bubble for 2 to 3 minutes, then remove from the heat, cover with a lid, and leave to cool.

When the cakes are baked, place the pans on wire racks and leave to cool for about 10 minutes. Now set a large tray or plate under the rack to catch any syrup that escapes. Spike holes all over the tops of the cakes with a skewer almost to the bottom and pour the syrup over the cakes slowly and carefully.

Either sandwich the cakes together with lemon curd or simply put one on top of the other. Deck the top with the slices of lemon and bay leaves from the syrup.

Lemon curd

Put 5½ tablespoons (scant ¾ stick) unsalted butter, cubed, 1 cup unrefined granulated sugar, and the grated zest and juice of 2 large organic lemons into a heavy-based pan and stir over low heat until the sugar is dissolved. Stir in 3 beaten large eggs. Keep stirring, taking care not to overheat, until thickened, 5 to 10 minutes. Seal in jars.

Butter cookies

These are a little on the slender side to be shortbread, I feel, so I call them butter cookies. They take only 5 minutes to make and are so much better than the commercial alternative. You can flavor the dough with a little grated orange zest and a few drops of orange oil, or chocolate chips if you prefer. Or, for the best summer version, finely chop 9 to 12 heads of lavender flowers and add them to the mixture. These lavender cookies are especially good served with ice cream. In early spring, you can use rosemary flowers in the same way for an unusual variation. Cut the dough into circles, half-moons, or hearts, as the mood takes you.

Makes 25 to 30.

1 cup (2 sticks) unsalted butter, cut into cubes

⅔ cup unrefined superfine sugar

2½ cups all-purpose flour

flavoring (optional, see above)

raw or turbinado sugar or a little unrefined confectioners' sugar, to sprinkle

Preheat the oven to 340 degrees F. Mix the butter, sugar, and flour briefly in a food processor until the mixture forms a dough that just coheres into a ball. Add any flavoring ingredient (as suggested above) at this point, and briefly work into the dough by hand.

Flatten the ball with your hand on a lightly floured work surface, then roll out to about a ¼" thickness. Use cookie cutters to stamp out the shapes you want.

Lift the shapes onto a greased baking sheet with a spatula, leaving a decorous gap in between. If you are using lavender or rosemary, press a short stem and its flower head gently into each one at this stage. If using raw sugar, sprinkle evenly on top.

Bake for 10 minutes before checking. They may need up to 5 minutes longer, but should be faintly colored around the edges.

Leave the cookies on the baking sheet for 5 minutes to firm up, then slide a spatula underneath and lift them onto a wire rack to cool. Sprinkle lightly with confectioners' sugar unless you have sugared them before baking.

There is a whole genre of food that rejoices in coming together under a single roof. The "one-pot dinner" is its name. Yes, you may wish to cook rice or potatoes to serve on the side, or an extra vegetable, but the whole point of a stew or tagine, a pasta bake or pilaf, a pot roast, daube, or braise is that you really have very little else to think about. Timing is not too much of the essence, it cannot spoil easily, and it is happy to fly solo. Lift the lid on it and you need look no further.

So the received wisdom of the day is that beef is bad, beef is red meat, beef is expensive. In these islands we traditionally eat beef only on Sundays. As far as I'm concerned, the prohibition gives me something valid to beef about. We know processed meats are bad for us, that sausages, bacon, salami, and cured hams should be eaten only in moderation. We know we shouldn't eat too much red meat. Producing it robs the earth of precious rainforest and water, and, as importantly, of more growing space for the humbler grains: rice, wheat, millet, corn; of the vegetables, cereals, and fruits that need scant acreage and water supply in comparison in order to feed a far greater population for far less money.

We have the answer, yet we ignore the question, the problem. How foolish we will look when people look back upon what we know now, and analyze why we were so resistant to do what was necessary for our survival, our health, and the continuance of the planet.

Proselytizing is going to get me nowhere, I know, but offering recipes that use the cuts of meat based on working muscle, skin, and

dinners

bone—the true providers of flavor and texture—in which the vegetables and grain are not mere counterpoint, they <u>are</u> the point, is what this chapter is all about.

Hock, belly, shank, marrowbone, oxtail, skirt, trotter, brisket, and cheek . . . What have we done to our cuisine by limiting it to "fast," no longer embracing "slow"? We have discarded some of the things we have cooked best of all throughout our culinary evolution, and now we are going to bring them back. Fiscal force majeure will see these classic cuts back on our plates, in our homes, and in our cookbooks—a reminder to people that chicken breasts are not the only meat.

The dos and don'ts of our eating etiquette seem to change daily and involve more rules than we could begin to count. So I stick to the simple rules of the table:

Pleasure comes first, but not at a cost to the environment, the animal, the farmer, or the pocket.

If you eat fewer processed foods you will automatically be eating better and for less, astonishing though that may seem.

Eat less and better and do less to your raw ingredients; this will make them taste more of themselves. The fewer and better quality the ingredients, the more vibrant and clear the flavors.

Entertain your friends royally, but be proud to do it with the humblest of ingredients.

Invite them to a "one-pot dinner." You really can't go wrong.

Beef stew with mustard and thyme dumplings

Chuck steak, stewed long and slow in a bottle of red wine, with some lovely fluffy golf balls of green-flecked dumplings steamed on top—a British answer to matzo balls. You may prefer parsley and horseradish in your dumplings, but surprise heat is a must, so either mustard or horseradish is necessary for bite and warmth.

Serves 6.

3¼ pounds chuck steak

about 2 tablespoons seasoned flour

2 tablespoons olive oil

2 large onions, peeled and chopped

6 garlic cloves, peeled and left whole

coarse salt and black pepper

4 celery stalks, strings removed with a potato peeler and sliced

4 large carrots, peeled and cut into chunks

2 large leeks, cleaned, whites cut into short lengths, green tops saved

1 small rutabaga, peeled and cut into cubes

1 small celery root, peeled and cut into cubes just before using (optional)

1 bottle robust red wine

14-ounce can whole tomatoes

a bouquet garni of parsley, thyme, rosemary, bay, and 2 strips of orange peel, tied together

for the dumplings

¾ cup (rounded) self-rising flour

2 ounces fresh beef suet, shredded or chopped

1 tablespoon thyme leaves, chopped, or 2 tablespoons chopped parsley

1 tablespoon whole-grain mustard or 1 teaspoon Colman's English mustard powder, or 2 teaspoons freshly grated horseradish

to serve

colcannon

Preheat the oven to 300 degrees F. Cut the beef into large cubes. Pour the flour into a Ziploc bag, add the meat, lock, and shake to coat. Take out the meat, shaking off excess flour. Heat about 1 tablespoon olive oil in a large, heavy-bottomed casserole, and brown the meat in batches all over, removing it to a plate when browned and adding extra oil as needed.

Add the onions and garlic to the pan and sprinkle with a little salt. After a few minutes, as they begin to soften, add the celery, carrots, leeks, rutabaga, and celery root, if using. Sauté for a few minutes and then return the meat to the pan. Meanwhile, heat the red wine to a simmer.

Add the canned tomatoes to the pan and chop them down into the meat and vegetables. When the liquid is bubbling away merrily, add the wine to just cover. Once the pot has come up to the bubble again, tuck the bouquet garni down into the depths, add a circle of waxed paper to just cover the stew and put the lid on. Transfer to the oven and cook for 2 hours or until the vegetables are tender but not reduced to mush.

Meanwhile, make the dumplings. Sift the flour into a large bowl and throw in the suet. Add the herbs, mustard or horseradish, and seasoning, and mix well together. Slowly add cold water, 1 tablespoon at a time, and mix with your hands or a spoon until the dough coheres but is not too wet and sticky. If it becomes too damp, scatter a little more flour over and roll the ball of dough gently. Flour your hands and pull small, walnut-size pieces of dough from the ball, rolling them between your palms into balls.

About 20 minutes before the stew will be ready, uncover and set the dumplings on top. Put the lid back on and return to the oven. After 20 minutes, check that the dumplings have swollen and are cooked through. A couple of dumplings per serving is enough for all but the hardiest and heartiest of eaters. Don't forget the colcannon.

Colcannon

Slice a small savoy cabbage into slim ribbons, add to a pan of fast-boiling water and cook for 5 minutes, then drain and refresh under cold water. Peel 6 medium potatoes, cut into chunks, and boil (as for mashing). Clean and finely chop the leek tops (saved from the stew), discarding any tough outer layer, and fry gently in butter until soft. Drain the potatoes and mash well, incorporating about ½ cup hot whole milk and 6 tablespoons (¾ stick) butter. Reheat gently, stir in the cabbage and buttery leeks, adjust the seasoning, and serve.

Brisket with pickled walnuts
and celery root

This really is a complex-flavored dish, robust with meat, nuts, and autumnal or winter vegetables. Celery root works brilliantly, but if you don't have any, add more celery and carrots, even some turnips, if you like a bitter twist. Please improvise if you don't have any stock on hand, and add a little more wine and some water instead.

Pickled walnuts are a British specialty and not widely available in the United States. But you can find recipes for pickling them on the Internet—especially useful if you are lucky enough to have a walnut tree in your garden. My tree is still a baby and not producing nuts yet; when it does, I will be on permanent squirrel alert.

Serves 6 to 8 (depending on the amount of vegetables).

3¼ pounds thin-cut beef brisket, rolled and tied

a little flour

coarse salt and black pepper

1 tablespoon beef drippings or olive oil

1 celery root

3 onions, peeled and roughly chopped

6 medium carrots, peeled and cut into chunks

3 celery stalks, strings removed with a potato peeler and sliced

6 garlic cloves, peeled

2¼ cups red wine and beef stock mixed, about half of each

8 pickled walnuts, halved, plus 3 tablespoons liquid from the jar

3 bay leaves

a sprig of rosemary

Preheat the oven to 300 degrees F. Sprinkle the fat side of the brisket with a little flour and season with salt and pepper.

Heat a large, heavy-bottomed casserole into which the brisket will fit snugly, and then add the drippings or olive oil. (If you are using drippings, add the jellied dark juices below the fat too, for flavor.) When the brisket is fizzing, put it into the pot, fat side down, and allow it to brown for 3 to 4 minutes, then roll it over and brown the meat all over. Remove the meat to a large plate.

Peel the celery root and cut into small chunks. Swiftly throw it into the pot with the onions, carrots, celery, and garlic and brown briefly on all sides, adding some salt and a good scrunch of pepper. (You need to prepare the celery root just before cooking, otherwise it will discolor.)

Meanwhile, heat the red wine and stock together in a small pan.

Skim off the excess fat from the surface, then put the meat back into the pot with the vegetables and pour in the hot red wine and stock. Add the pickled walnuts with their liquid and the herbs and bring slowly to simmering point.

Cut out a circle of waxed paper and lay it over the surface, then cover with the lid. Put the pot in the oven and cook for 2 hours before peeking and testing the vegetables and meat. It may take another 30 minutes for the meat to feel tender and the vegetables to be cooked through.

This dish can be made with chuck steak cut into large pieces, about 2½" square and ¾" thick. Brown in the same way and then cook as above at a lower temperature, 275 degrees F, for 4 hours.

Oxtail stewed with grapes

This is one of those dishes that are somehow jocund, beneficent, and fruitful, and I simply have to make it at least once a winter. It is a heart-and-soul dish with the lovely autumnal feel of the vineyard, where it is served in France at the end of the grape harvest. I have never known anyone, however tail-shy, not to assault it with gusto, and love the coarse-textured grapey sauce with its sweetness and depth of flavor. This recipe is adapted from one by the late well-known British cookery writer Elizabeth David.

It is worth making it with at least two oxtails, or three, as it will both freeze and keep well in the fridge for a few days, and is great reheated.

Please start the day before, if you have time, so that the dish can cool and chill and you can then scrape the fat off and put the sauce through a food mill.

Serves 6 to 8.

2 oxtails, chopped by your butcher

¼ pound pancetta, cut into small strips

2 large onions, peeled and chopped

4 large carrots, peeled and cut into small dice

2 celery stalks, strings removed with a potato peeler and chopped

6 garlic cloves, peeled

a bouquet garni of bay, parsley, rosemary, thyme, and a strip of orange peel, tied together

coarse salt and black pepper

2 whole allspice berries

about 2½ cups red wine

2 pounds seedless green grapes

Preheat the oven to 275 degrees F. Have the oxtail cut into pieces and ready to cook. Throw the pancetta into a large, heavy-bottomed casserole and scatter the chopped vegetables and whole garlic cloves on top. Get the cooking process started over low heat, so that the fat starts to run from the pancetta. Once it's all fizzing merrily, put the pieces of oxtail on top of the vegetables and bury the bouquet in their midst. Season and add the allspice, then pour enough wine over to just cover. Bring to a simmer before throwing in the grapes.

Cut out a circle of waxed paper and lay it over the surface as the liquid comes back up to simmering point. Cover with the lid and cook in the oven until tender, about 3 to 4 hours, though longer won't harm. You can serve the dish right away, but it is best left to cool, then refrigerated overnight.

The following day, spoon off the solidified white fat from the surface and remove the meat to a plate. The liquid will have jellied delectably in the fridge. Discard the bouquet garni, then push the sauce through the coarse disk of a food mill. If you do not have a food mill, I suggest a quick blend in a food processor, though it won't give you the uniformly coarse sauce that really gives this dish character. Check the seasoning and return the meat to the casserole with the sauce. Reheat slowly and simmer for a few minutes.

Serve in warm soup plates—the moat of sauce is what makes it—with just some mashed potatoes on the side; you don't need another vegetable.

Braised side of pork with quince

Pork and apricots, pork and apple, pork and prunes . . . We know and love the sharp, soft fruits that add taste and acidity to the rich sweetness of pork, but what, I thought, about pork and quince? My quince tree hasn't yielded a solitary "Aphrodite's apple" yet, but the farmers' market has them in the autumn, and then later in the winter they arrive from North Africa with the pomegranates, and how glad we are just to scent a room with one on a mantlepiece or poach them in syrup.

This dish works miraculously, the pork and the fruit infusing and informing one another with a special magic. And the quinces should be turned to tenderness when the meat falls from its little rib bones.

Serves 4.

3 pounds (approx.) fresh skin-on pork picnic shoulder, ideally organic, scored

1 to 2 tablespoons olive oil

coarse salt and black pepper

2 quinces

juice of 1 lemon

2½ cups good, dry hard cider

1 heaping tablespoon blackstrap molasses

3 bay leaves

1 star anise

6 juniper berries, bruised

2 cloves

1 tablespoon muscovado or dark brown sugar

1 tablespoon acacia or other clear honey

Preheat the oven to 275 degrees F. Lay the pork, rind up, on a board. Rub some olive oil into the rind with your fingers, then do likewise with salt and pepper. Leave the pork to stand in a cool place for 30 minutes to 1 hour.

Heat a little olive oil in a heavy-bottomed casserole and add the pork, skin side down. The rind should seize and brown a little. Slide a knife under the skin into the fat at intervals to encourage it to run a little.

Quarter the quinces, leaving their skins on, and core them. They will be very hard, so go carefully with the knife. Instantly dunk them all over in the lemon juice so that they don't discolor.

Take the pan off the heat and tuck the quinces snugly around the pork. Heat the cider and pour it around the quinces and meat. Drip the blackstrap molasses over the pork, throw in the bay leaves, star anise, juniper berries, and cloves, and sprinkle with the sugar and honey. Bring back to a simmer. Cover with a circle of waxed paper, cut to fit, and the lid. Cook in the oven for 2 hours.

Spike a quince quarter to see that it is tender; if not, return to the oven and test again after another 20 minutes.

Serve straight from the pot. I like to serve mine with cranberry beans—soaked and cooked in half red wine and half water—with added cubes of celery root fried in olive oil and rosemary. Potatoes or brown rice would also be good.

Sausage and mustard casserole
with cabbage and chestnuts

One of those lovely dishes where you simply cannot imagine the alchemy of the final result from the commonplace ingredients you know so well.

This dish is based on Jane Grigson's "cabbage in the Troo style"—named for the Provençal village where she has a home. I fell in love with its utterly unpretentious marriage of pork and cabbage, whose juices flooded, the one into t'other, and, with the aid of a little butter and much slow cooking, resulted in a patty of pink and green layers of succulent beauty.

I have added coarse-grain mustard from Gascony to mine and a wintry, mealy, rubble of chestnuts to the cabbage, but you can leave them out if you like. This is a dish of substance and will just need a baked potato besides.

Serves 4.

6 good pork sausages

1 savoy or other green cabbage

coarse salt and black pepper

2 heaping teaspoons whole-grain mustard

12 to 15 whole, peeled, cooked organic chestnuts, broken in half

large knob of butter, about 2 tablespoons

Preheat the oven to 275 degrees F. Skin the sausages. Put a large pan of water on to boil. Thinly slice the cabbage; wash and drain. When the water is boiling, throw the cabbage in, press it under the water, and bring back to a boil. Boil for 3 minutes, then drain immediately in a colander and pour cold water over to refresh it and arrest the cooking process. Press out as much water as you can.

Grease a small casserole with butter and add a third of the cabbage. Season lightly (the sausages should be well seasoned). Press three of the sausages flat between your hands and place them on top of the cabbage to create a complete layer. Spread the mustard over the sausage. Add another third of the cabbage along with the chestnuts. Flatten the rest of the sausages to create another layer, then top with a final layer of cabbage.

Dot with butter and cover the surface with a sheet of waxed paper and then the lid. Bake for 2 to 2½ hours; longer won't hurt if you are playing for time.

Serve with baked potatoes.

Orange-scented lamb
with chickpeas, rice, and yogurt

I have long been an admirer of Afghani cuisine, albeit through a single tome, the delightful
Noshe Djan *by Helen Saberi. The ingredients are accessible and inexpensive and the cuisine
is not harshly or pungently spiced. In this dish the gentle scent of orange peel and turmeric
wafts through with the dill as it comes to fruition.*

*It is a great stride away from the Mediterranean and Middle Eastern cuisines, which we
have absorbed and taken to our hearts over the last 50 years—which is, I feel sure, what drew
me to it originally. It isn't like anything else I know. It is a cuisine of strength, simplicity,
complexity of flavor and depth, marrying meat with rice, yogurt, and legumes—chickpeas,
mung beans, split peas—and with dried fruits—dates, apricots, prunes.*

*This is a late autumn and winter dish, everything cooked in a single pot and only a salad
needed besides.*

Serves 6.

1¾ pounds, or thereabouts, lamb shoulder on the bone, cut into 3 large hunks

3 medium onions, peeled and finely sliced

1 teaspoon ground turmeric

1 large orange, sharp rather than sweet

coarse salt and black pepper

2 cups short-grain rice, washed and drained

2 cups Greek-style live-culture yogurt

4 garlic cloves, peeled and smashed with the flat of a knife blade

1 tablespoon olive oil

1 tablespoon chopped fresh dill or 2 teaspoons dried

2½ cups cooked chickpeas, drained (see page 28; canned if necessary)

Preheat the oven to 275 degrees F. Put the chunks of meat into a large, heavy bottomed casserole with the sliced onions. Add enough water to cover. Sprinkle with the turmeric and bring to a simmer. Cover with a circle of waxed paper, cut to fit, and the lid. Cook in the oven for 3 hours or until the meat is tender and falls easily from the bones. Alternatively, cook gently on the cooktop over very low heat, checking after a couple of hours.

While the meat is cooking, pare the zest from the orange. Cut it into matchstick strips and leave to soak in warm water.

When the meat is tender, remove it from the pot and tear into long thin shreds by hand, discarding the bones. Return the meat to the pot, season, and add the rice. The liquid should cover the rice by about ¾", so add more water if needed. Bring to a boil, then reduce the heat to a simmer and cook with the lid off, stirring from time to time, until the rice is *al dente* and the liquid is absorbed. You may need to add a little extra water as the rice is cooking.

Add the yogurt, stirring it in thoroughly.

In a small pan, sauté the garlic in the olive oil until pale golden, then add to the meat and rice. Drain the orange peel and add it, too, along with the dill and chickpeas. Mix all together and check the seasoning. Cover with the lid and leave on very low heat for 30 minutes to allow the flavors to marry.

Lamb and kidney pudding
with a rosemary crust

I'm particularly pleased with this new dish. An old-fashioned suet crust is quick, easy, and satisfying to make, yet so often overlooked on the basis that it is too heavy. Well, this turned out crisp and not too heavy, golden brown with flecks of rosemary, and the filling sealed inside imparted every last burst of intense flavor. The wine-dark gravy gave a whiff of kidney and garlic, a hint of red currant. I ate three helpings.

As for the cooking, it really couldn't be easier. Shunt the pudding in the oven in its bain-marie and forget about it for 2 to 2½ hours. If you have the time, start the dish early so you can cool the filling before pouring it into the crust.

Serves 4 to 6.

1 pound boneless lamb shoulder, trimmed of fat

3 lamb's kidneys, skin removed, halved and cored

1 tablespoon seasoned flour

1½ tablespoons finely chopped rosemary needles

2 tablespoons olive oil

1 onion, peeled and minced

3 garlic cloves, peeled and sliced

1½ tablespoons red currant jelly

1¼ cups robust red wine

coarse salt and black pepper

for the suet crust

2 cups (slightly rounded) self-rising flour

2 ounces fresh beef suet, finely chopped or shredded

1 teaspoon baking powder

1 level tablespoon finely chopped rosemary needles

cold water to mix

Cut the lamb and kidneys into small cubes. Place the seasoned flour and 1 tablespoon chopped rosemary in a Ziploc bag. Add the lamb and kidney, lock, and shake to flour, then take out, shaking off excess flour.

Heat 1 tablespoon olive oil in a wide, heavy-bottomed pan and throw in the rest of the chopped rosemary needles. When they fizz, after about 30 seconds, add the onion and garlic and sauté until the onion begins to soften and turn translucent. Remove to a plate with a slotted spoon.

Add the rest of the oil to the pan and fry the lamb and kidneys until browned all over. Add the red currant jelly and melt, then pour in half the wine. Let it bubble and reduce before adding the rest. Cook for 3 minutes, then season. If the juice looks too thick, add more wine. Remove from the heat and allow to cool completely, if you have time.

Make the crust just before using. Preheat the oven to 350 degrees F. Mix the dry ingredients in a large bowl. Season and stir in 3 tablespoons cold water to begin with, then 1 tablespoon at a time, until the dough forms a ball. Flatten on a floured surface, then roll out to a large circle that will line a 1¼-quart capacity heatproof bowl. Cut out a quarter for the lid.

Ease the three-quarter circle into the greased bowl, leaving some overhang, and press the straight edges together. Roll out the quarter piece to make a circle for the lid. Spoon the filling into the bowl and top with the lid, pressing the edges together to seal and trimming as necessary. Cover with a sheet of waxed paper, topped with a sheet of foil, first making a pleat in the middle of the combined sheets to expand with the steam. Tie string tightly around the rim, making a loop for easy removal.

Put the bowl into a large casserole and pour in enough boiling water to come halfway up the side. Put the lid on and steam in the oven (or on the cooktop) for 2 to 2½ hours; it is not fussy time-wise.

Lift the pudding out and remove the paper lid. Leave for a few minutes to settle. Run a spatula around the outside of the crust and then invert the pudding onto a hot serving dish—deep enough to contain the gravy. Serve with mashed potatoes and cabbage.

Chicken or rabbit savory cobbler
with bell peppers and tomatoes

Chicken and rabbit can both handle strong accompanying flavors, so celery, red onion, garlic, tomatoes, and roasted bell peppers are all in the picture, as are paprika and fruity olive oil. Garlicky sausage is included, too, but you can leave it out if you prefer.

A crisp and fluffy crust of light biscuits, scented with thyme and Parmesan, adds substance and is a good alternative if you feel like a spud-less supper. Note that cobblers need to be served hot so that the "cobbles" don't lose their crispness and become sodden.

Serves 6.

4 red bell peppers, or use roasted piquillo peppers from a jar (wood-roasted are ideal)

3 to 4 tablespoons olive oil

1 large chicken, cut up, legs and thighs separate, each breast in two; if using rabbit, see note

1 large red onion, peeled and minced

3 or 4 garlic cloves, peeled and sliced

3 celery stalks, strings removed with a potato peeler and chopped

a bouquet garni of 3 or 4 sprigs of thyme, 2 bay leaves, and 2 strips of orange peel, tied together

1 pound coarse, garlicky sausage, cut into chunks (optional)

14-ounce can diced tomatoes

½ to 1 teaspoon paprika

coarse salt and black pepper

for the biscuits

1½ cups all-purpose flour

2 level teaspoons baking powder

6 tablespoons (¾ stick) chilled unsalted butter, diced

4 tablespoons freshly grated Parmesan or sharp Cheddar, plus extra to sprinkle

6 sprigs of thyme, leaves stripped and chopped

¾ cup light cream or milk

Preheat the oven to 350 degrees F. Char the red peppers all over under a hot broiler, or by holding with a pair of tongs over a gas burner, then place in a bowl, cover with plastic wrap, and leave for 5 minutes or so (the steam will loosen the skins). Peel the peppers while still warm, remove the core and seeds, and cut into strips.

Heat half the olive oil in a heavy-bottomed ovenproof casserole and brown the chicken or rabbit pieces on all sides over medium heat. Remove them to a plate.

Add the rest of the olive oil to the pan and sauté the onion, garlic, and celery until just beginning to soften, then add the bouquet garni. Throw in the sausage chunks, if using, and brown on all sides briefly.

Return the chicken to the pan and add the tomatoes and strips of red pepper. Sprinkle with the paprika and season with salt and pepper. Bring to simmering point, then cover with a lid and cook in the oven for 20 minutes.

Meanwhile, make the biscuits. Sift the flour and baking powder into a large bowl and rub in the butter lightly and quickly with your fingertips, then stir in the grated cheese and thyme. Add the cream or milk and mix with a fork until the dough coheres.

Flour your hands and shape the dough into little biscuits, about 2" in diameter and ½" thick. Plop them on top of the stew, sprinkle a little extra grated cheese over, and return to the oven. Cook, uncovered, for another 40 minutes or until the biscuits have swollen and turned golden and crisp.

Leave to stand for 10 minutes before serving.

If you are using rabbit: to serve 6 you really need to ask your butcher for an extra couple of legs. Cut up the whole rabbit into 2 back legs and split the saddle in two.

Pheasant braised with endive,
white wine, and crème fraîche

This dish works just as well with guinea fowl, and in season the lovely garnet-colored Treviso radicchio to offset an otherwise ivory dish. The sauce is sharpened with crème fraîche and lemon juice and the endive sweetened with a little dark brown sugar. No other vegetable is needed, though you may like to serve it with green beans and mashed potatoes.

Serves 4.

2 tablespoons olive oil

4 tablespoons (½ stick) unsalted butter

2 cut-up pheasants, legs on the bone, breasts whole

coarse salt and black pepper

8 heads of Belgian endive or Treviso radicchio, or half of each

1 onion, peeled and minced

1 level tablespoon dark muscovado sugar or dark brown sugar

juice of 1 lemon

1 cup (scant) white wine

1 cup crème fraîche

a handful of flat-leaf parsley, minced

Heat the olive oil and butter together in a heavy-bottomed casserole. Add the pheasant pieces, skin side down, and cook until golden brown, then turn to brown the other side and season with salt. Remove to a plate with a slotted spoon.

Throw the endive heads into the pot with the onion and sugar and cook for about 5 minutes, turning them to color all over. Add the lemon juice and return the birds to the pot. Pour in the wine, bring to a boil, and allow it to simmer for a few minutes.

Pour in the crème fraîche and season with pepper. Cover the surface with a circle of waxed paper, cut to fit, and put the lid on. Cook at a gentle simmer for 30 to 40 minutes or until the pheasant juices run clear when you insert a skewer through the thickest part of the meat.

Pour the sauce off into a small pan, keeping the meat and endive hot in the covered pot. Let the sauce bubble for a few minutes to thicken and reduce slightly.

Return the sauce to the pot, add the minced parsley, and serve on heated plates.

One-pot fish pie
with spinach and leeks

The thing about a good fish pie is that it's not just as good as the cost of the fish you put in it. You can add raw scallops, shrimp, mussels, clams, with cod, hake, or haddock as chief fish, but there is nothing wrong with less expensive white fish spruced up with a little smoked haddock, a layer of spinach and some leeks and frozen peas. Cut your cloth, or fillet your fish, according to your purse. This really is a one-pot wonder, too—the base of spinach and the seam of leeks and peas in béchamel allow you to serve it alone and not even offer another vegetable unless you want to.

Serves 6.

2 pounds tilapia or other white fish, filleted

½ pound finnan haddie fillets

1 bay leaf

2½ cups whole milk, heated

3 or 4 fat leeks, cleaned

4 tablespoons (½ stick) unsalted butter

2 tablespoons all-purpose flour

½ cup dry vermouth or white wine

coarse salt and black pepper

nutmeg for grating

1½ pounds or thereabouts spinach, well washed

a few shellfish if your budget can stretch to it, such as cleaned raw scallops (one each) or cooked shrimp, mussels, or clams (2 or 3 each)

¾ cup frozen peas

2 tablespoons chopped dill or half parsley, half dill

for the topping

6 large potatoes, peeled

a little hot milk

several knobs of butter

Preheat the oven to 400 degrees F. Lay the white fish and finnan haddie fillets, skin side down, in a large, greased au gratin dish. Add the bay leaf and pour the hot milk over. Bake for 10 to 15 minutes until opaque (or cook gently in a shallow pan on top of the stove for about 10 minutes). In the meantime, boil the potatoes for the topping in the usual way.

While the fish is cooking, make the béchamel sauce. Thinly slice the green part of the leeks and chop the white part into chunks. Melt the butter in a large pan, toss in the leeks (green and white), and stir them around for a few minutes. Scatter in the flour and stir. Once the fish is cooked (it should be by now), pour off the milk into a pitcher. Gradually stir the fishy milk into the leeks, then add the vermouth or wine, stirring over the heat until the sauce is thickened and smooth.

Season the sauce with salt and pepper and grate some nutmeg over. Cook gently, stirring from time to time. Meanwhile, break the fish into large chunks, discarding the skin; set aside on a plate.

Drain the potatoes when they are tender and mash with hot milk and some of the butter.

Cook the spinach, with just the water clinging to the leaves after washing, for 2 to 3 minutes until it has just wilted. Drain, adding the small amount of liquid to the sauce. Spread the spinach over the bottom of the au gratin dish and season with salt and pepper.

Scatter the flaked fish over the spinach, along with any extras, like disks of raw scallop or cooked, shelled shrimp, mussels, or clams. Add the frozen peas to the leek béchamel, stir for a few minutes, then remove from the heat. Add the herbs and adjust the seasoning, then pour the leek béchamel over the fish.

Top with the mashed potatoes, rough up the surface with a fork, and dot with little knobs of butter. Bake for 25 minutes or until browned on top and bubbling at the edges.

Autumn vegetable lasagna

This is not strictly vegetarian, but it can be if you want it to be. Nor is it strictly an autumn dish; you just need to tweak the vegetables in the rootier direction if zucchini are in the past tense, and add butternut squash, red bell peppers, celery root, eggplants, or what you will. If the morels are beyond your budget, eschew them, likewise the prosciutto; but you need so little of both, and the morels, with their bosky fungal liquid, contribute so much depth of flavor, that it is worth stretching a financial point if you can. I like the combined forces of pecorino and Parmesan scattered over this dish, but if you have only one or the other, don't worry.

Serves 4.

2 tablespoons olive oil

½ pound cremini mushrooms, sliced

¾ ounce dried sliced morels, soaked in warm water to cover for 30 minutes and drained (optional)

2 tablespoons Marsala or port or Madeira (or red wine if you have a bottle open)

3¾ cups whole milk

1 bay leaf

4 tablespoons (½ stick) butter

2 tablespoons all-purpose flour

coarse salt and black pepper

nutmeg for grating

1 large onion, peeled and minced

2 medium-size garlic cloves, peeled and sliced

6 small green or yellow zucchini, cut into small cubes

14-ounce can diced tomatoes

a handful of basil leaves, torn

6 slices prosciutto, sliced into long strips (optional)

14 ounces good-quality dried lasagna (preferably not no-need-to-precook type)

5 tablespoons each of freshly grated Parmesan and pecorino

Preheat the oven to 400 degrees F. Heat 1 tablespoon of the olive oil in a small pan and cook the sliced cremini mushrooms until they begin to release their juice. Add the morels with their soaking liquid, if using, and the Marsala, and simmer for 5 minutes. Remove from the heat.

To make the béchamel sauce: heat the milk with the bay leaf in a pan. Melt the butter in another pan, stir in the flour, and cook for a minute or so until you have a pale brown roux, then add a quarter of the hot milk and whisk until smooth. Continue to add the milk, a quarter of it at a time, whisking well. Season and flavor sparingly with nutmeg. Add the liquid from the mushrooms and let the sauce cook gently for another 15 minutes, stirring from time to time. Adjust the seasoning.

Meanwhile, sauté the onion and garlic in the remaining olive oil with a sprinkle of salt until they begin to soften, then add the zucchini cubes and cook until they are *al dente*. Add the tomatoes and torn basil and simmer the mixture for 10 minutes. Season with pepper.

Add the mushrooms to the béchamel. Heat the prosciutto strips briefly in the pan used to cook the mushrooms, with no extra oil, turning until they begin to crisp a little, then add to the mushroom sauce mixture.

Cook the lasagna sheets (if necessary), according to the package instructions, until *al dente*, then drain in a colander.

Spread a little béchamel, avoiding the additions, over the bottom of a large baking dish, then add a layer of lasagna sheets. Cover with half of the remaining béchamel mixture. Add another layer of lasagna, followed by the zucchini and tomato mixture. Add a final layer of lasagna and the last of the béchamel mixture. Top with the grated cheese.

Bake for 30 minutes or until golden and bubbling, and when a skewer inserted in the center meets with little resistance from the lasagna. Leave to stand for 10 minutes before serving; this is one of those dishes that seem to stay hotter for longer.

If you find the zucchini and tomato mixture is somewhat more than you need for the single seam of brightness through the middle of your lasagna, keep the mixture for a pasta sauce to make a something-out-of-nothing supper (page 175).

Happy food

A life without treats is unthinkable. Treating ourselves, being spoiled—an unfortunate phrase for something we all desire and deserve; spoiling the ones we love is more often than not just cooking or eating the food that makes us happy. It should be guilt-free but it rarely is; pleasure, greed, and guilt, are, after all, major contributors to our sense of well-being and wickedness, and are all part of the fun.

When we are broke, we need to reward ourselves more than ever, with little luxuries in the absence of large ones. On "high days and holidays," on broken-heart days and midwinter-blues nights, at teatime, on birthdays, on cold, sullen, rainy days, any days, we need cheering-up, mood-altering substances like chocolate, cream, strawberries, cherries, butter, and bread.

Good home-baked bread straight out of the oven, crisp, caramelly crusted, and warm within—sliced with cold, salty butter or sweet unsalted French or Italian butter—well, I could happily live on it if I had to choose one food and one alone, though it would be a tough call between bread and potatoes.

A garlicky, creamy dauphinois, or a steaming bowl of smooth-as-silk buttery mashed potatoes? I'd have to toss a coin between those two. Crisp roast potatoes ruffled with a fork and turned in hot goose fat—the ultimate indulgence. What else? A bitter-sugar-topped crème brûlée, a wobbly panna cotta dotted with vanilla, crème caramel with praline, or some rich vanilla ice cream with a dark chocolate sauce that seizes, freezes, and sets on top of it.

Thinking about food always makes me happy. But it isn't quite enough. It's not all about cream and butter; a lot of it is about simple pleasures, such as a ripe white Italian peach or nectarine, a wild strawberry, or dark cherries on a white plate.

As I write this, in a cold-snap of winter, drifts of snow against the door, the track to the house impassable, the fruit cage so weighted with last night's snowfall that it has collapsed like the broken hull of a ship dashed on rocks in a storm, I am savoring a bowl of Japanese squash gnocchi—starchy and satisfying, slippery with butter and snipped sage, showered in their own snowstorm of Parmesan and pecorino (page 168). Pure comfort food that makes me happy. Even the color is a happy color. When the gnocchi bob to the surface of the simmering water like miniature lifebuoys, it's as though the sun has just come up.

Thinking about food is so much about remembering the first time a particular dish or ingredient infused you with happiness. If only I could revisit some of those memories, go back to Alba for a bowl of homemade buttered taglierini with grated white truffle and nothing else, with a scent so bewitching it could be the aroma of the devil telling me more, more. Yes, food memories are a great source of happiness: the time, the place, the people one ate the particular dish with.

And chocolate: cure-all, seduce-all chocolate. Good chocolate never fails. A chocolate espresso cake, an assortment from La Maison du Chocolat, Fran's smoked salt caramels in dark chocolate—one bite and the caramel explodes in your mouth with a final note of salt upon the tongue.

Here are some recipes that I hope will make you happy, too. They may bring back memories or inspire new ones.

White chocolate and raspberry truffles

There is almost as much pleasure in skewering these cold raspberries and twirling them in chocolate, fondue-style, as there is in eating them, but I will leave you to find that out for yourselves. Any child can do it, and if you can't be bothered to make a more conventional dessert, these will please every bit as much.

Makes about 30 to 35.

2 cups raspberries

½ pound good white chocolate (not chips)

up to 1 scant tablespoon unsalted butter

Put the raspberries on a plate in a single layer in the freezer for 30 minutes.

Melt the chocolate in a double boiler or in a heatproof bowl set over a pan of simmering water, but not touching the water.

Remove the pan from the heat, keeping the melted chocolate over the warm water. Drop a couple of tiny knobs of butter into the chocolate to stop it from seizing.

Spike a skewer through a raspberry and dip it into the chocolate until it is enrobed completely. Place the truffle on a foil-lined tray to set. Continue with the rest of the raspberries. If the chocolate seems to be hardening, add another few tiny knobs of butter and 1 teaspoon boiling water to help thin it, stirring both in.

When you have finished, put the tray of truffles in the fridge until the chocolate has completely set.

Chocolate and chestnut terrine

This is the perfect dessert, with a lovely fondant texture to the chocolate and a lighter, creamier chestnut layer to complement it. Nothing complicated, it is so worth making, and much, much easier than the end result suggests. You can make the terrine in advance and keep it in the freezer for a few days, if you need to.

Don't use canned chestnut puree; it always seems to taste metallic. If you can't find the puree in jars in your supermarket, try the Internet. Sierra Rica organic sweet chestnut puree in a jar is wonderful.

Line a terrine or loaf pan, approx. 9 x 5 x 3", with plastic wrap, allowing enough overhang to cover the top later. Break off about one-fifth of the chocolate (reserving this for grating) and melt the rest gently in a double boiler or heatproof bowl set over a pan of simmering water, making sure the bowl is not touching the water. Once the chocolate has melted, remove the bowl from the pan.

Meanwhile, dissolve the sugar in the water in a heavy-bottomed pan over medium-low heat. Bring to a boil and simmer for 10 minutes or until you have a syrupy consistency. Do not boil rapidly, otherwise the syrup will reduce too much and overthicken, becoming difficult to work into the egg yolks.

While the syrup is simmering, whisk the egg yolks thoroughly using an electric mixer; I do this for 3 to 4 minutes. Pour the hot syrup in a steady stream onto the egg yolks, then whisk for about 10 minutes or until the mixture has dramatically increased in volume and turned pale, light, and fluffy.

Whip the cream in a bowl until it holds soft peaks. Add the kirsch and whisk it in briefly. Empty the sweet chestnut puree into a large bowl and scrape the melted chocolate into another.

Using a large metal spoon or spatula, fold half of the whipped cream into the chestnut mixture followed by half of the whisked egg and sugar mixture.

Fold the remaining half of the whipped cream and half of the whisked egg and sugar mixture into the chocolate mixture.

Scrape the chocolate mixture into the prepared terrine or pan and smooth over the surface with a rubber spatula. Scrape the chestnut mixture lightly and carefully onto the chocolate and smooth over. Cover with the overhanging plastic wrap and put in the freezer for at least 6 hours, or overnight, or for a few days if you are preparing ahead.

Remove from the freezer 20 minutes before serving. Turn the terrine out onto a plate and peel away the plastic wrap. Grate or scrape curls of chocolate over the top, and if you have them, add some chestnuts in syrup, broken by hand, around the terrine.

Serves 8 to 10.

5 ounces dark chocolate, 64 to 72% cocoa solids

²/₃ cup superfine vanilla sugar

½ cup water

5 organic large egg yolks

1¼ cups heavy cream

2 tablespoons kirsch

9-ounce jar sweet chestnut puree

to finish

4 or 5 chestnuts in syrup, to finish (optional)

Rich chocolate truffle cake

Sometimes one wants rich. A small slice of something utterly dazzling, which for me with chocolate has to be something on the critically rich list. Yes, there is a lot of chocolate and a lot of cream in this recipe, but a little goes such a long way that this is not a financially out-of-bounds dessert. You don't need to use a very expensive chocolate either. I used Menier's and it was decidedly good enough.

Also, since you can make this truffle cake in minutes and it doesn't even have to hit the oven, it is time, cost, and energy efficient. Not that good chocolate ever needs such an excuse. Just tell yourself there is no butter, flour, or sugar in it, if you need to feel a modicum of virtue.

Serves 10.

1 pound dark semisweet baking chocolate, 64 to 74% cocoa solids

2½ cups heavy cream

cocoa powder for sprinkling (I use Green & Black's)

Line an 8" cake pan as well as you can with plastic wrap, allowing the edges to drape over the rim so that it won't shoot down into the pan when you pour in the chocolate mixture.

Break the chocolate into bits and melt in a double boiler or in a large heatproof bowl set over a pan of barely simmering water, making sure the bowl is not touching the water. Every so often, stir the chocolate a little as it melts.

In the meantime, warm the cream in a pan, but do not let it get hot. When the chocolate has melted, remove the top of the double boiler or the bowl from the pan and stir in the cream off the heat.

Pour the chocolate and cream mixture into the cake pan and allow it to cool, then put it into the fridge to firm up for 4 hours or so, or until the truffle cake is clearly no longer at all wobbly.

Remove from the fridge and lift the cake out of the pan. Hold an overturned serving plate over the top—a white plate always looks good for a dark chocolate cake—then turn over, so that you have the smooth underside on top. Sprinkle the cake with a thin layer of cocoa powder and return to the fridge.

Remember to take the cake out of the fridge 15 minutes before you intend to eat it. You may like to serve it with cream whipped with a little confectioners' sugar and 1 tablespoon cooled, very strong espresso whisked in. Or you may just serve it alone or with a few raspberries on the side.

Baked bitter chocolate custards

I have made this dish from a standing start, as it were, when inviting people to dinner at the last minute and thinking, Help! I must make a "dessert"! It is pretty much a pantry recipe.

A blackberry compote and a homemade blackberry sorbet (page 159) are happy partners—the warm and cool and chill work well—but these custards can stand alone perfectly.

Serves 4.

¼ pound dark chocolate

¼ cup heavy cream

1 tablespoon freshly made strong coffee, cooled to tepid

1 cup (scant) whole milk

4 organic large egg yolks

¼ cup unrefined superfine sugar

Preheat the oven to 300 degrees F. Melt the chocolate together with the cream in a double boiler or a heatproof bowl set over a pan of gently simmering water.

As the chocolate melts, stir in the coffee. Remove from the heat and whisk in one-third of the milk.

Whisk the egg yolks in a separate bowl, then whisk in the sugar until the mixture is pale and creamy. Whisk in the rest of the milk. Pour in the chocolate mixture and fold together, using a spatula, until evenly combined.

Pour the chocolate mixture into 4 ramekins, dividing it equally between them. Stand the ramekins in a roasting pan and surround with enough boiling water to come halfway up their sides. Bake for about 25 minutes or until the custards have set.

Remove the ramekins from their bain-marie and let the custards cool to warm before serving.

Date and coffee sponge cake
with a coffee glaze

Instant gratification is hard to come by without resorting to chocolate, but here is a lovely, quick-to-make cake that I've decided belongs in this chapter because it is a cake with a difference. It can be a pudding, too. With its intensely coffee-flavored, not-too-sweet crackle top, it is such a delight. Use Medjool dates to make it taste really special, but any date will do. This is a cake to eat with coffee, too.

Serves 8 to 10.

¾ cup (1½ sticks) butter

1 tablespoon freshly ground coffee

5 tablespoons boiling water

2 organic large eggs

¾ cup light muscovado sugar or light brown sugar

1½ cups (scant) all-purpose flour

2 level teaspoons baking powder

½ cup whole milk

1 cup pitted dates, chopped into quarters

for the glaze

1 cup (scant) unrefined confectioners' sugar

1½ tablespoons butter

2 tablespoons strong coffee (from above)

2 to 3 teaspoons boiling water (if needed)

Preheat the oven to 300 degrees F. Grease an 11 x 7" baking pan or pan with similar dimensions, about 2" deep.

Melt the butter in a small pan and set aside. Make the coffee using the 5 tablespoons boiling water, strain, and set aside 2 tablespoons for the glaze.

Whisk the eggs using an electric mixer. Add the muscovado (or brown) sugar, flour, baking powder, melted butter, milk, and 2 tablespoons coffee. Whisk until amalgamated, then fold in the dates by hand. Pour the mixture into the prepared pan, making sure the dates are evenly distributed.

Bake for 30 minutes or until a skewer inserted into the middle comes out clean. Place the pan on a rack to cool the cake slightly while you make the glaze.

For the glaze, place the confectioners' sugar in a bowl. Melt the butter and, while it is still hot, pour onto the confectioners' sugar, followed by the reserved 2 tablespoons coffee. Stir until smooth. The consistency should be thick, so that you know the glaze will set as it cools. If it seems too thick, add 2 to 3 teaspoons boiling water to thin.

Pour the glaze over the cake in the pan and smooth gently with a spatula. There will be just enough to cover the cake; this is not a thick frosting.

If you can restrain yourself from cutting the first slice until the frosting has cooled and set, good for you.

Cardamom and orange crème caramel
with nut brittle

It is often the simplest old "slippers" of dishes, the well-worn, tried, and tested old favorites, that give the most pleasure, either made as they have always been made or revamped a little with a twist of the new. This is one of those. It is a real shoestring of a dessert, too, and you will usually have the ingredients on hand.

Orange and cardamom are perfect bedfellows, and served with tempting brittle, this is as comforting as anything milky or creamy can be. Satin textured, it slips and slides on the plate and delivers that lovely combination of sweet creaminess and bitter nuttiness. You won't be able to resist breaking off shards of brittle to eat solo either, so consider doubling the quantity.

Serves 6.

½ cup superfine vanilla sugar, plus 2 tablespoons

1 tablespoon cold water

2 organic large eggs, plus 2 extra yolks

1 vanilla bean, split, seeds scraped and removed

2½ cups whole milk

6 cardamom pods, cracked open to expose the seeds

a few drops of sweet orange oil

finely grated zest of 1 orange

for the nut brittle

¼ cup each pistachios, hazelnuts, and almonds

½ cup superfine vanilla sugar

Preheat the oven to 300 degrees F. Have ready an 8 to 8½" soufflé dish. Gently melt the ½ cup sugar in a heavy-bottomed skillet until it is liquid and has turned a burnished mahogany color. Just as it starts to bubble, throw in the 1 tablespoon cold water and instantly pour the caramel into the soufflé dish. Tilt and turn the dish so the caramel coats the base and partway up the sides as it sets.

Whisk the eggs, extra yolks, 2 tablespoons sugar, and the vanilla seeds together in a bowl. Slowly heat the milk in a pan with the empty vanilla bean and cracked cardamom pods to just below a boil. Immediately pour it onto the egg and sugar mixture, whisking as you do so, then add the orange oil and zest. Cover and leave to infuse for 10 minutes.

Strain the mixture onto the caramel base. Place the soufflé dish in a roasting pan and pour in enough boiling water to come two-thirds of the way up the side. Cook in the oven for 1½ to 2 hours or until you can see the custard has set. It should still be a little wobbly in the middle.

Leave the dish in the bain-marie to cool the crème caramel slowly, then chill in the fridge for a few hours.

For the brittle, chop the nuts very slightly. Scatter the vanilla sugar over the base of a heavy-bottomed pan and heat it to a burnished mahogany color (as for the caramel). Throw in the nuts, stir for a few seconds, making sure the nuts are completely covered with the caramel, then pour onto a greased baking sheet and allow to set firm.

To turn the crème caramel out, run a spatula cautiously around the edge of the dish, place an overturned deep plate—that will hold the liquid caramel—over the top of the dish, and invert it carefully. Bash the brittle up a little to serve with the caramel.

Bitter chocolate sorbet

A shot of espresso intensifies this near-black sorbet, which feels rich to the tongue with cocoa, although there isn't a drop of cream in it. I think for an exuberant effect, it should be served alongside a panna cotta (such as the one opposite), together with some raspberries, but better a solitary scoop of sorbet than no dessert at all.

Serves 6 to 8.

½ pound dark chocolate, 64 to 72% cocoa solids

2 tablespoons cocoa powder (I use Green & Black's)

2 tablespoons freshly made espresso, cooled to tepid

1 cup (scant) unrefined granulated sugar

2½ cups water

Break up the chocolate and place it in a heatproof bowl with the cocoa powder and espresso.

Put the sugar and water into a heavy-bottomed pan and dissolve over medium-low heat, stirring. Bring to a boil and then continue to boil the sugar syrup for 5 minutes.

Remove from the heat and pour the sugar syrup over the broken chocolate and cocoa powder, stirring as you do so until the chocolate has completely melted. Allow to cool to tepid.

Pour the mixture into an ice-cream machine, if you have one, and churn until set, or freeze in a suitable container, whisking every hour for the first 3 hours to break down the ice crystals.

Either serve the sorbet right away or keep it in a sealed container in the freezer, taking it out about 15 minutes before you wish to serve it to allow it to soften slightly. It really is best eaten within a week.

Piedmont panna cotta

More of that milky, creamy thing that always seems to satisfy, and is cool and elegant. The traditional panna cotta from Piedmont, in Italy, has a burst of pêche de vigne *liqueur in it. If you do not have any, use an eau-de-vie from another fruit, such as prune, pear, quetsche, kirsch, raspberry, or marc, instead, or just add a nuance of orange flower or rose water, if you'd rather. This dessert is all about texture and cool smoothness, so little speckles of vanilla are enough if you want it booze-free and not like a scented bough!*

Panna cotta is often served alongside sugared and macerated fresh berries or a fruit compote, depending on the season. A lovely idea, but do keep the flavors separate—this is not about raspberry coulis poured over panna cotta.

Serves 6.

1¾ cups heavy cream

⅔ cup whole milk

1 vanilla bean, split, seeds scraped

⅓ cup (generous) superfine vanilla sugar

1 tablespoon (1 envelope) powdered gelatin

3 tablespoons cold water

⅓ cup boiling water

2 or 3 tablespoons pêche de vigne or other fruit eau-de-vie (optional)

Oil 6 ramekins or dariole molds, using almond oil or another tasteless oil.

Put the cream, milk, vanilla seeds, and empty bean in a heavy-bottomed pan, add the sugar, and heat slowly until the sugar dissolves. Simmer gently for a minute, keeping a watchful eye on the pan, then take the pan off the heat. Cover and leave the mixture to infuse as it cools. Remove the vanilla bean.

In a small dish, sprinkle the powdered gelatin over the 3 tablespoons cold water and let it soften for 2 minutes. Add the boiling water and stir until dissolved.

Strain the cream mixture into a bowl, then add 2 tablespoons of it to the gelatin, stirring rapidly. Now add the gelatin to the cream mixture, stirring thoroughly to dissolve it. Add the eau-de-vie or other flavoring, if using, at this point. You want a scent, not an overwhelming taste of alcohol.

Pour the mixture into the oiled dishes and allow to cool. Cover with plastic wrap and refrigerate for at least 2 hours or until set.

To serve, run a knife around the edge of each panna cotta and turn out onto individual plates.

You can use gelatin leaves or sheets instead of powdered gelatin. They vary in size considerably, so check the package instructions for recommended quantities and setting capacities.

General satisfaction

This lovely Victorian nursery pudding is addictive, like a comfort blanket, and delectable in equal measure. And with a name like this, happiness is clearly its heartland. Those old-fashioned ladyfingers, which are a good store-cupboard stand-by for a trifle or syllabub, are made jammy, custardy, and meringuey. That's all there is to it.

Serves 6.

1 level tablespoon cornstarch

1¾ cups whole milk

1 vanilla bean, split, seeds scraped

3 organic large eggs, separated

½ cup superfine vanilla sugar, plus 3 tablespoons

1 cup (rounded) apricot, raspberry, or strawberry jam

1 teaspoon water

12 to 15 ladyfingers

a little oloroso or palo cortado sherry, to sprinkle (optional)

Preheat the oven to 350 degrees F. In a small bowl, mix the cornstarch with 1 tablespoon of the milk.

Pour the rest of the milk into a small, heavy-bottomed pan and add the vanilla seeds, empty bean, and blended cornstarch. Bring to a boil, stirring, and simmer, still stirring, for a couple of minutes. Remove from the heat.

Whisk the egg yolks in a bowl, then whisk in the hot milk. Return to the pan and whisk over low heat until the custard thickens and is perfectly smooth; don't let it boil. Remove from the heat and whisk in 2 tablespoons sugar. Leave to cool.

Gently melt the jam with the 1 teaspoon water until runny and pour it over the base of a medium baking dish. Lay the ladyfingers on top and sprinkle with a little sherry, if using. Strain the cooled custard through a sieve over the ladyfingers.

Whisk the egg whites until stiff, then whisk in the ½ cup sugar, 1 tablespoon at a time, to make a firm, shiny meringue. Spoon the meringue over the custard and sprinkle the final spoonful of sugar on top.

Bake on the middle shelf of the oven for about 20 minutes until the meringue is pale gold on top and crisp when you tap it. Serve warm.

Tiramisu

Pudding snobbery is something I abhor. Yes, a tiramisu is the Italian answer to trifle, but there is nothing intrinsically wrong with that. It may have got something of a bad name from poor factory-made imitations. At best it is a dish of lovely textures and flavors, of hidden depths and subtlety, and when made with the best ingredients, just happens to be one of my favorite desserts.

This particular version combines everything I know that is the secret to happiness. Ignore it if you are a miserabilist; make it the day before you want to eat it if you want untold pleasure.

Serves 6.

1 organic large egg, plus 3 extra yolks

¼ cup white wine

¼ cup Marsala

2 tablespoons Amaretto di Saronno (or use cognac and a few drops of natural almond extract)

½ cup superfine vanilla sugar, preferably unrefined

½ pound mascarpone

1 teaspoon instant espresso coffee powder or 1 tablespoon strong black coffee

for the sponge base

1¼ cups espresso coffee or strong black coffee

1½ tablespoons superfine vanilla sugar

2 tablespoons Marsala

30 to 32 ladyfingers, or amaretti cookies

to finish

2 level tablespoons dark cocoa powder (I use Green & Black's)

Whisk together the egg, egg yolks, white wine, Marsala, and Amaretto in a double boiler or in a bowl set over a pan of simmering water, making sure the bowl is not touching the water. Continue to whisk until the mixture becomes a thick and frothy zabaglione.

Remove from the heat and whisk for another couple of minutes. Add the sugar and let it dissolve. Gently fold in the mascarpone with the coffee powder or liquid until the mixture lightens to a cream.

For the base, mix together the espresso, sugar, and Marsala in a shallow dish. One by one, briefly dip half of the ladyfingers into the espresso mixture, on both sides, so that they absorb the liquid but do not break up. Immediately lay them, side by side, in a large, shallow serving dish.

Spoon half the zabaglione mixture over the ladyfingers. Repeat with another layer of ladyfingers, placing them at right angles to the first layer; this helps the tiramisu to hold together when you serve it.

Cover with the rest of the zabaglione and sift over this far more cocoa powder than looks sensible. It needs to well and truly cover the surface, not be a mere dusting. Cover and refrigerate, ideally overnight, until ready to serve.

Tartiflette

This is midwinter mountain food, for both on and off the piste, and as close as it gets to comfort and joy. Eat it at the top of the mountain and you will be a little closer to heaven naturally. It is also what your body craves to carry it through the exertions and cold of the afternoon ahead. But don't worry if you're a lowlander; as long as the weather is harsh, the time is right for a tartiflette.

The inimitably creamy, fruity tang of Reblochon, a cheese from the French province of Savoy that is as brilliant as Comté for cooking with, is what makes this simple dish quite as pleasurable as it is.

Serves 4.

1½ pounds potatoes, peeled
coarse salt and black pepper
5 ounces bacon or pancetta
1 medium onion, peeled
4 tablespoons (½ stick) butter
½ cup warmed white wine
½ Reblochon (¾ pound)

Preheat the oven to 375 degrees F. Boil the potatoes in salted water until not quite soft. Meanwhile, cut the bacon into strips and slice the onion into fine rings. Throw the bacon into a pan of boiling water and blanch for a minute, then drain and pat dry. Drain the potatoes and let them cool to the point where you can hold them, then cut them into ½"-thick slices.

Melt half the butter in a large, heavy-bottomed skillet and throw in the bacon and onion. Stir to coat in the butter and cook over a gentle heat for 10 minutes or so, until the onion is softened and pale gold. Add the sliced potatoes and the rest of the butter and cook gently, trying not to let the potatoes break up. After 4 or 5 minutes add the warm wine and continue to cook for 5 minutes.

Scrape the contents of the pan into a greased au gratin dish. Cut the Reblochon horizontally through its middle and put each half, rind-side down, on top of the potato mixture. Bake for 20 to 25 minutes or until the cheese has formed a lovely sticky crust on top.

Leave to stand for 5 minutes before serving—with a baguette and a plain green salad with a mustardy dressing.

Ham and Comté cake

You know that feeling before dinner when you just need a little something salty to wake up the taste buds and see you through to dinner, and you don't want to drink without eating. On a recent trip to the Franche-Comté, where the great Comté cheese is made, I was told that this "cake" has become the fashionable French tidbit to serve with an apéritif. It is known simply as "le cake." It takes minutes to make and can include any spare ham or bacon, green or black olives, a little thyme, even some dried tomatoes (page 161). A glass of wine—from the Jura, to be faithful to the region—is all you'll need with it.

Makes 10 to 12 slices.

1½ cups all-purpose flour

1¼ cups grated Comté or Gruyère

5 ounces ham or pancetta, cut into small pieces

⅓ cup chopped, pitted olives

6½ tablespoons (¾ stick) butter, melted

2 or 3 sprigs of thyme, leaves stripped and chopped

3 organic large eggs

1 to 2 tablespoons milk

2¼ teaspoons quick-rise dry yeast

coarse salt and black pepper

Preheat the oven to 400 degrees F. Butter a loaf pan, approx. 9 x 5 x 3".

Put the flour, cheese, ham, olives, butter, thyme, eggs, milk, yeast, and seasoning into a large bowl and mix well. Scrape into the prepared pan.

Bake for 10 minutes, then turn the oven down to 350 degrees F and bake for another 20 minutes or until risen and browned. Insert a skewer into the center to check that it is cooked through; it might need a few minutes longer. There may be some bubbling butter on top of the cake at this stage. If so, just pour some of it away; the rest will be reabsorbed into the cake as it cools.

Leave in the pan on a wire rack to cool for 20 minutes, then turn out and eat warm. Any leftover cake will keep well for a few days wrapped in waxed paper and foil. Just cut off the outside slice, which may have dried a little, each time.

Use your loaf

I am the worst culprit. I argue that throwing bread to the birds is not wasting it. I cut my crust to suit my cloth, which inevitably results in end bits and heels, cut-off crusts, and leftover slices. Sometimes I make bread for the sheer pleasure of making it, not because I need it. Need doesn't come into it. I window-shop a good loaf in the way some people window-shop for clothes. If I spy a new baker, some particularly beautiful, distinguished-looking bread, if I get the scent of good dough, I will buy two, three, four loaves, to try them all. Reality sets in when I get home. It goes against the grain to cut a slice from each one of them. Now which do I freeze and which do I tuck into now?

A good loaf has both beauty and irresistibility. I find I can never deny myself, and that goes for brioches and croissants, too. I am on a continuous search for the best loaf, the best crust, the lightest, egg-rich, yeastiest brioche that just pulls away when you tear it, that is warm enough and sweet enough and dry crusted to perfection. Pull off its little beret first and eat it whole with cold French butter.

And then there is the croissant: flaky, buttery, yet not greasy, substantial, yet ethereal. Maybe a second one. Maybe butter on top too—though the French would never do it. And the search for the best apricot jam, for that is the best match for both, the croissant and the brioche, I can't resist a good loaf. Or brioche. Or croissant.

I am determined to mend my ways: to eat up my crusts and cook and freeze to the last stray slice. To bake rolls more often, so I can freeze, then unfreeze them—one by one, or two by two. To make smaller loaves, to slice and freeze, to turn to crumb or chunk and leave not even the mouthful my father would always leave on the edge of his plate. "Papa, why have you left that bit of bread?" I always asked, and the answer was always the same: "For the little people." An Irish expression for the fairies, it's a part of my childhood memory of food and will live with me always.

Bread is the easiest and most satisfying of foods to use up— even, or rather particularly, when it is stale. It takes on a new life, new hope, new invention when stale, and there aren't many things in life one can say that about. It is possibly the most versatile ingredient in the world, when fresh, when stale, whenever. We can make salads, soups, and stuffings with it, and sauces for vegetables, fish, and chicken. We can make French toast and traditional English puddings. We can bake bread and sauté bread, dry bread and dunk bread. We can do much the same with stale brioche and croissants—we just need a pinch of spice and imagination, of fruit and eggs and milk and sugar, and our daily bread is reincarnated.

If there is any better, more evocative scent in the world than that of bread baking, bread cooling—yeasty, crusty, savory, sweet—I have yet to smell it. I promise I will not waste bread.

Making bread

Lay the myth to rest. Practice makes perfect, yes, but anyone can make bread, and the time involved is about waiting—not working, not difficulty. The end result is so worth it in my book. And bread is easy to make in bulk and freeze if you can get into the groove. I buy organic flour in bulk and get my fresh yeast for next to nothing from the bread counter at any supermarket bakery.

These loaves call for around 10 minutes of good arm-wrestling work to stretch the gluten, but getting the dough started the night before takes only as long as it takes to fill a hot water bottle and really isn't any more complicated. The slow fermentation means that the flavor and the digestibility of this bread are unequaled by any quick-rise method.

the night before

½ cup (generous) lukewarm water

a piece of compressed yeast, the size of a walnut

1 cup (scant) stoneground whole-wheat bread flour

the next stage

1lb whole-wheat or half whole-wheat, half white bread flour

⅜ cup (scant) organic all-purpose flour

a handful of toasted bran and wheat germ (optional)

2 teaspoons coarse salt

1 tablespoon organic blackstrap molasses

1 tablespoon organic malt syrup (if you don't have any, use 2 tablespoons molasses)

1 tablespoon olive oil

1 to 1¼ cups lukewarm water

semolina to sprinkle

beaten egg to glaze

1 tablespoon each poppy, sunflower, and sesame seeds, or any combination (optional)

The night before, or at least 12 hours ahead, pour a generous half cup of lukewarm water into a measuring cup and add the yeast. Agitate with a fork until it has dissolved.

Put the flour into a bowl, pour on the warm, yeasty liquid, and mix with a fork until combined; the bowl needs to be big enough for the dough to triple in volume. Cover the bowl with plastic wrap and leave at room temperature. Go to bed!

The next day, put the flours and wheat germ mix into a really large bowl and add the coarse salt, molasses, malt syrup, and olive oil. Scrape the previous night's sticky dough on top. Add 1 generous cup warm water at this stage and work with your fingers until the mixture coheres. You will probably need to add more of the warm water.

Place the dough on a lightly floured surface and work, kneading with your fingers and occasionally stretching out the dough—unfurling it with the heel of your hand, then rolling it back toward you. Keep this up for 10 minutes, then put the dough back into the large bowl and cover the bowl with a damp dish towel. Leave the dough to rise until it has doubled in size; this will take an hour or so.

Next, scatter semolina evenly over a large baking sheet. Either divide the dough into a dozen or so rolls or into two small loaves or form it into one large loaf. Place the bread on the baking sheet, spacing rolls apart. Cover with a huge plastic bag, forming a tent that doesn't touch the dough.

Preheat the oven to 425 degrees F. Leave the dough to rise in a warm place, perhaps near the oven, for 15 to 20 minutes.

Uncover the dough and brush with egg glaze. Throw some seeds or extra semolina on top if you feel like it. Place on a higher oven shelf, with enough ceiling space for the dough to rise. Bake in the oven for about 40 minutes for a single loaf, but check at 30 minutes, and again at 35 minutes, if the crust is looking brown. A pair of loaves should be checked at 25 minutes but will probably take 30 minutes. Rolls will need only 15 to 20 minutes. To test, tap the underside with your knuckles: the bread will sound hollow if it is cooked through. Immediately remove to a wire rack to cool.

Resist eating until it is only just warm, as still-steaming bread will make the interior crumb damp. Holding back really is the most difficult part of the whole process.

If for any reason you decide not to bake the dough on the day, after kneading you may hold it in the fridge overnight again, in a covered bowl. Then take it out of the fridge and give it two hours to rise.

Pa amb oli, pa amb tomàquet

Literally (from the Catalan) "bread and oil, bread and tomato." My old schoolfriend Tomas Graves, son of the poet Robert, wrote a whole book about the subject, *Bread and Oil, Majorcan Culture's Last Stand*. Tomas grew up and still lives on Majorca. The Catalonians simply call the dish *Pa amb tomàquet*; they don't mention the oil. You need—simply—good bread, good olive oil, coarse salt and garlic to taste, and good tomatoes.

The tomato is sometimes just squashed and rubbed onto the bread after the garlic and olive oil, or sometimes placed on top in chunks or slices. The wet tomato juice is the whole idea. This is made with good country bread, ideally cooked in a wood-fired oven, so a day old, a few days old, no matter; it is still a good loaf. The lubrication is what this dish is all about.

You may add a few anchovies or olives, you may lightly toast the bread, as in Italian bruschetta, before the rubbing commences and then sprinkle oregano over the tomato, if you like. This way of not wasting crumb or crust is a natural accompaniment to a drink or a soup, or can serve as an appetizer in its own right. Salt it at the end, onto the tomato. Children on Majorca often sugar it.

Summer panzanella

If I were to say "stale bread salad," would you turn the page and think, "No, how unappealing"? "Stale" has these dreary, derogatory connotations—as Shakespeare acknowledged when Hamlet cries,

> *"How weary, stale, flat, and unprofitable*
> *Seem to me all the uses of this world."*

Yet stale is good. All the uses of the loaf are nothing if not profitable and delicious when stale and weary—and sometimes even flat. Have you ever dampened and grilled stale pita bread and torn it into a Greek salad, sprinkling it with good, young feisty olive oil as you go? Perhaps added a little halloumi, also grilled? What a lunch!

Serves 6.

4 best large ripe tomatoes

2 cucumbers

1 red onion, peeled, halved and sliced into thin half-moons

4 or 5 tablespoons really good fruity, peppery olive oil

coarse salt and black pepper

1 small, dried, fairly hot chile, seeded and minced

6 thick slices stale, good country bread, crusts removed

2 to 3 tablespoons iced water

2 tablespoons aged red wine vinegar

a small handful of basil leaves, torn

1 level tablespoon tiny capers, rinsed and drained

To peel the tomatoes, first spike them with the tip of a knife, then immerse in a bowl of boiling-hot water for 30 seconds to loosen the skins. Immediately drain and refresh under cold water—you don't want them to cook. Pry out the core with the tip of a small knife, then peel away the skin. Halve and seed the tomatoes, then chop chunkily, saving the juices.

Peel the cucumbers, quarter lengthwise, and scoop out the seeds with a teaspoon. Cut the cucumbers into sticks.

Combine the tomatoes, cucumbers, and onion in a large bowl and toss together with your hands. Pour in 4 tablespoons fruity olive oil to start with, add the dried chile, and season with salt and pepper. Toss again, adding a touch more oil if you think it is needed, then leave for an hour or so to let the flavors get acquainted with each other.

In the meantime, preheat the oven to 310 degrees F. Lay the slices of bread on a baking sheet and toast them in the oven until pale golden and crisp, turning halfway through; this may take up to 30 minutes. Dampen them a little with the tomato juice. Put a slice of toast on each serving plate, or arrange them on a large platter.

Just before serving, pour 2 to 3 tablespoons iced water and the wine vinegar over the salad in the bowl and toss well. Pile on top of the toasted bread and scatter the torn basil and capers over the salad.

Winter panzanella

Here is the Italian version. My winter Italian version because the turn of the year is the time for lovely garnet- and cream-leaved Treviso radicchio and pale, bitter endive, which add so much color and flavor to a winter dish. And in winter, cooked and raw can work together so well. Salads are not always appealing in the cold months. Add bread, add something cooked, and you will find yourself seduced.

Serves 4.

1 red bell pepper, or use good roasted piquillo peppers from a jar (wood-roasted are ideal)

1 small red onion, peeled

2 heads of Treviso radicchio

1 Belgian endive

1 very thick slice stale, good white country bread, crusts removed

a handful of cherry tomatoes or dried tomatoes (page 161), halved

3 or 4 anchovies, chopped

1 tablespoon capers, rinsed and drained

a handful of good olives (tiny black Taggiasca or giant green Mammuth are my favorites here), pitted and sliced

6 to 8 basil or sage leaves

for the dressing

a splash of olive oil

a drizzle of red wine vinegar

black pepper

If using a fresh red bell pepper, char it all over under a hot broiler, or by holding it with a pair of tongs over a gas burner, then place in a bowl, cover with plastic wrap, and leave for 5 minutes or so (the steam will loosen the skins). Peel while still warm, then remove the core and seeds. Cut the roasted pepper into broad strips.

Slice the red onion as thinly as you can, preferably using a mandolin. Halve the Treviso and endive vertically and chop a few chunks from their base at the same time. Throw everything into a large, colorful salad bowl as you go.

Tear the bread into large chunks and lightly run cold water over each chunk, then squeeze it out inefficiently, so that it is still damp as you toss it into the bowl. Add the tomatoes, roasted red pepper, anchovies, capers, and olives, and some torn basil or sage leaves.

Dress the salad sharply. I add the olive oil first and then the wine vinegar, holding my thumb across the open mouth of the vinegar bottle. Salt is unnecessary with anchovies, capers, and olives, but a scrunch of pepper is good. Toss the salad with your hands, please, it seems to help the flavors mingle and marry.

Best served 30 minutes or so after making—after another toss and taste and adjustment of oil and red wine vinegar if necessary.

Fried mozzarella sandwich

Mozzarella in carozza, or "mozzarella in a carriage," is a classic snack, but, as such, should not be the victim of poor ingredients—inferior bread and mozzarella. A ball of fresh mozzarella di bufala is, to my mind, essential for this dish. As is good country bread or ciabatta, eggs, and olive oil. Enough said. I sometimes accompany mine with tomato chile jam (page 162), which I'm sure Campanians would consider sacrilegious.

Serves 4.

8 slices good country bread

1¾ pounds mozzarella di bufala, sliced

coarse salt and black pepper

1 cup (scant) whole milk

2 organic large eggs

a handful of all-purpose flour

olive oil for shallow-frying

Sandwich the bread slices together in pairs with the mozzarella slices, dividing the cheese equally and seasoning with salt and pepper before you close them.

Pour the milk into a shallow bowl that you can sink the sandwiches into flat. Beat the eggs with some seasoning in another similar bowl. Throw a handful of flour onto a large plate and spread it evenly.

Pour ½" of olive oil into a skillet, large enough to take a couple of the sandwiches, and heat over medium-high heat until hot but not smoking.

Meanwhile, dip two of the sandwiches into the milk briefly, then into the flour, shaking off any excess, and then into the egg mixture, again letting any excess drip back into the bowl.

Fry the sandwiches in the hot oil until they are golden brown on both sides, turning them once. Remove and drain on paper towels; keep warm while you fry the other two. Serve at once.

Racing eggs

My cousin Deborah and I share a greed, fascination, and love of good food, originally inspired by the wonderful cooking we enjoyed at our grandparents' home. We cook similarly, though often dissimilar things, so it's always exciting to swap notes and ideas. Last year she invited me to the races at Cheltenham. As usual, with Deborah, nothing was ready-made for the picnic. Even if you have no interest in horses, you can bet this is a recipe that will delight all ages on a picnic. I couldn't stop eating them.

Makes 12.

2 slices stale white or brown bread, crusts removed

1 teaspoon chopped thyme leaves

1 tablespoon finely chopped flat-leaf parsley

12 quail eggs

½ pound good-quality pork sausage meat

2 scallions, trimmed and minced

3 teaspoons chopped chives

2 organic large (hen's) eggs

coarse salt and black pepper

a handful of seasoned flour

sunflower or peanut oil for frying

Preheat the oven to 300 degrees F. Process the bread with the thyme and parsley in a blender to fine crumbs, then spread out on a baking sheet and dry in the oven for about 15 minutes.

Put the quail eggs in a small pan of cold water, bring up to a boil, and then simmer for just 3 minutes to hard-boil them. Drain and cool immediately under cold running water, then shell them carefully.

Mix the sausage meat with the scallions, chives, and 1 beaten egg. Season, remembering that sausage meat is salty. Divide into 12 equal pieces. Scatter the seasoned flour on a plate.

Roll a quail egg in the flour, shaking off any excess. Flatten a piece of sausage meat with your hands and wrap it around the egg to enclose it completely. Repeat with the rest of the quails eggs.

Beat the remaining egg on a plate and put the herbed bread crumbs onto another plate. Dip the sausage-coated eggs first into the beaten egg mixture, then into the herbed crumbs to coat them thoroughly and evenly. Set aside on a plate.

Heat 1½" of oil in a large, heavy-bottomed skillet to 350 degrees F or until a cube of bread dropped into the oil turns golden brown and fizzles in less than a minute. Lower the eggs into the oil and fry, turning carefully and frequently, for 3 to 4 minutes, until browned. Drain on crumpled paper towels. Eat just warm or cold.

Soup with bread, or bread with soup

Recently I have started making a different soup almost every day with whatever I've got hanging around, not always relying on stock. Strong, vibrant flavors can come from herbs and spices, from roasting vegetables, rather than cooking them in water, from adding garlic, cheese, a sharp cooking apple. It's amazing quite how big and bold a potage you can build with really very little.

One day I roasted carrots, parsnips, and garlic in olive oil with thyme and liquidized them with water. Another day I used up a slightly sad-looking cauliflower by roasting it with red onion, blending again with water, and finishing the soup with smoked paprika and saffron, dunking in a little yogurt at the end.

I've made carrot soup with a baked apple tossed in and a crumble of salt blue cheese to sharpen the sweetness. And broccoli soup, heavy on the onion, made with half whole milk, half water, with sharp Cheddar grated in at the blending stage.

One outstanding soup came from a fried leek, onion, and potato base, to which I added red chile, lemongrass, garlic, cilantro, and half a block of creamed coconut with hot water. Roasted and raw can work magic together, too, as in the beet soup on page 106.

Often when I have leftover legumes, I make a soffritto of chopped onion, garlic, celery, and celery leaves, blend half with water, leaving the rest chunky, and sprinkle with olive oil, parsley, and Parmesan to finish. When the cupboard is all but bare, I will forge a garbure of savoy cabbage and potato, adding only water, seasoning, and the pureed cloves from a poached head of garlic.

I find using bread or potato as a thickener in a soup, instead of flour, gives it better body and flavor. Sometimes I will throw a cold baked potato into what otherwise would be a slightly gutless soup, or I add a spoonful of chestnut puree, or puree some of the beans, if it is a beany soup. I want floury and thickened, without the soup tasting floury and thickened, and this is the way to do it.

Think of the summery bread-based Spanish soups like gazpacho (page 109)—cooling, refreshing, and packed full of raw flavor.

The more I make soup, the less I resort to enriching with cream and butter. I prefer the simple, strong, earthy taste and texture of the basic ingredients to speak for themselves.

Pancotto or bread soup

All over Italy people make this soup with good Pugliese, or country bread, so that the result is not gluey. I love this cuisine, which salutes the loaf and uses crumb and crust for soups and pastas. Anna Del Conto, the great Italian food writer, says there are as many versions of this as there are cooks. This is one of hers.

Serves 4.

4 slices stale, good country bread, crusts removed

5 tablespoons best extra-virgin olive oil

½ teaspoon crushed dried chiles

3 garlic cloves, peeled and chopped

2 tablespoons chopped flat-leaf parsley

1½ quarts hot chicken stock

coarse salt and black pepper

freshly grated pecorino to serve

Tear the bread into small pieces and blend in a food processor for a few seconds, or chop coarsely.

Put the olive oil, dried chiles, garlic, and parsley into a heavy-bottomed pot and sauté for 30 seconds. Add the bread and cook, stirring frequently, for 3 to 4 minutes until it begins to turn pale brown. Add the hot stock, then cover and simmer for 30 minutes.

Taste the soup and adjust the seasoning if necessary. Serve with a bowl of grated pecorino cheese for sprinkling on top.

Mushroom soup with spices and bread

Use portobello or cremini mushrooms here, as they are flavorsome enough to hold their own and define the soup. Whole-wheat bread is used to add body. If you are using water instead of stock, you really need to include the leek and garlic for flavor.

Serves 4.

1 to 2 tablespoons olive oil

1 small red or white onion, peeled and minced

2 sprigs of thyme, leaves stripped and chopped

1 leek, green and white parts, cleaned and chopped (optional)

1 garlic clove, peeled and sliced (optional)

coarse salt and black pepper

1 pound mushrooms, cleaned and sliced

½ to 1 teaspoon ground ginger

3 or 4 juniper berries, slightly crushed with the back of a knife

3 or 4 tablespoons sherry, Marsala, Madeira, or red wine, depending on taste and what you have available

about 1 quart hot chicken stock or water

1 thick slice stale whole-wheat bread, crusts removed, torn into chunks

Heat the olive oil in a large, heavy-bottomed pot and add the onion and thyme, along with the leek and garlic, if using them. Sprinkle a little salt over and sauté gently until the onion has begun to soften.

Add the mushrooms and stir. Sprinkle over ½ teaspoon ground ginger and the bruised juniper berries. Sauté over medium heat until the mushrooms have first become dry and then begun to release their juices. At this stage, add the alcohol and let it bubble and become absorbed into the mushroom liquor. After 3 or 4 minutes add the hot stock or water and bring to a boil.

Cover with a lid, turn down to a simmer, and cook gently for about 10 minutes, by which time the mushrooms should have softened enough. Remove from the heat, season, and taste. The ginger should give warmth but not be too obtrusive. Add a little more if you need to.

Using a blender, liquidize ladlefuls of the soup with chunks of bread until smooth. Keep some soup and sliced mushrooms back to add bite and texture. Stir the pureed soup back into the pot. Taste and adjust the seasoning. The soup should not be stand-a-spoon-in-it thick, but it should have body.

Roasted and raw
beet soup with rye

The sweet earthiness of beets with their brilliant hue is such a great thing in the dark night of the soul-food winter. Splash it garishly into soups and citrussy goat- or sheep-cheese salads. It works roasted whole or cut into chunks, or grated raw.

This is my latest discovery: deep, dark rye marrying with the intense flavor of roasted beets and the color and crunch of the raw. A dollop of yogurt and a sprinkle of chopped tarragon or dill and you're there. Roast the beets ahead and the soup takes no time to make.

Serves 4.

4 or 5 medium beets, cleaned and trimmed, their whiskers left on

1 tablespoon olive oil

1 small red or white onion, peeled and minced

1 small garlic clove, peeled and minced

coarse salt and black pepper

1 quart plus 1 cup hot chicken stock or water

1 thick slice stale, good black rye bread, crust removed

a little good live-culture yogurt to finish

1 teaspoon finely chopped tarragon or dill

Preheat the oven to 400 degrees F. Wrap each beet separately and tightly in a piece of foil, except for the one you are going to grate in raw at the end. Roast in the oven for about an hour until cooked. To check, unwrap and pierce with a skewer through to the center; it should meet with little resistance. Peel the beets as soon as they are cool enough to handle and cut them into chunks.

Meanwhile, heat the olive oil in a large, heavy-bottomed pan and add the onion and garlic. Season with a little salt and sauté over medium heat until softened.

Add the roasted beet chunks, followed by the hot stock or water. Bring to a simmer and cook gently, uncovered, for no more than 5 minutes. You want this part of the cooking process over as quickly as possible so that the beets retain their vibrant color.

Remove from the heat, season with black pepper, and add the rye bread. Using a blender, puree the soup in batches. The texture should be thick, yet not too thick. If in doubt, add another ladle of hot stock to thin the soup down a bit. Check the seasoning.

Grate the remaining beet coarsely. Pour the soup into warm soup plates and spoon the grated beet into the middle. Top with a spoonful of yogurt and a sprinkle of chopped tarragon or dill.

Gazpacho

This soup predates Roman times, and there are said to be as many recipes for it as there are pestles and mortars. It is traditionally accompanied with little bowls of chopped egg, peppers, olives, onion, and ham, for everyone to scatter over their bowls what they will.

If you have time, make the gazpacho the night before you'll need it, and refrigerate overnight for the flavors to develop. If you make it at the last minute, you can put it in the freezer for 30 minutes to chill it quickly.

Serves 6.

1 pound ripe, flavorful tomatoes, or organic canned tomatoes if you can't get good fresh ones

2 small cucumbers

2 slices stale, good white country bread, crusts removed

1 small onion, peeled and cut into chunks

2 garlic cloves, peeled and chopped

2 tablespoons good peppery olive oil

coarse salt and cayenne pepper

1½ red bell peppers, quartered, cored, and seeded

2 tablespoons sherry vinegar

about 2½ to 3½ cups ice-cold water

Roughly chop the tomatoes if you are using fresh ones, leaving the skin on and seeds in. Peel the cucumbers, quarter lengthwise, and scoop out the seeds with a teaspoon, then cut into big chunks.

Hold the bread under cold water, then squeeze out the water gently and plop the chunks into the food processor with the onion, garlic, olive oil, 1 teaspoon salt, and a knife-tip of cayenne. Blend briefly to a pulp.

Add the cucumbers, red peppers, sherry vinegar, and tomatoes and blend to a coarse rather than a pureed texture. Pour the mixture into a large bowl, then cover and chill for several hours or overnight in the fridge, or quickly in the freezer.

Just before serving, dilute the soup with the ice-cold water, stirring and tasting until you have the flavor and texture you like. Adjust the seasoning and serve in tall glasses or soup bowls.

Spanish chicken
with a saffron and almond sauce

This lovely Moorish dish has been made over the centuries in Spain, but I discovered it only recently. It is so good I cooked it for everyone who came to stay last summer in Ireland, but it tastes just as good in the winter, the sauce thickened with fried bread—perhaps a little more than for the summer version. Add a heap of saffron rice or some new potatoes—the choice is yours—and something green besides. The color and texture of the sauce may not be beauteous, but please overlook that fact and judge it on flavor alone.

Serves 6.

1 large chicken, about 4½ to 5½ pounds, cut up into 8 pieces (see below)

1 cup hot chicken stock

36 or so whole blanched Marcona almonds

good pinch of saffron threads

2 to 3 tablespoons olive oil

3 garlic cloves, peeled and thinly sliced

1 thick slice stale, good bread, crusts removed

coarse salt and black pepper

pinch of grated nutmeg

2 cloves, crushed

½ cup fino sherry

a sprig of bay leaves

leaves stripped from 4 sprigs of thyme

1 tablespoon chopped flat-leaf parsley

spritz of lemon juice

Have the chicken pieces and stock ready. Preheat the oven to 300 degrees F. Scatter the almonds on a small baking dish and toast in the oven for 5 to 10 minutes until golden, keeping an attentive eye on them, as nothing browns faster than nuts. Discard any deep brown ones, as they will taste bitter and burned. Set aside.

Soak the saffron threads in a ladleful of the hot chicken stock in a small bowl.

Heat 2 tablespoons olive oil and the garlic slices gently in a large, heavy-bottomed skillet until hot; do not let the garlic brown. Remove it with a slotted spoon when the oil is hot and set it aside on a plate. Fry the bread in the garlicky oil on both sides until crisp and browned, and then remove it to the garlic plate.

Season the pieces of chicken well and sprinkle with a little freshly grated nutmeg and the crushed cloves. Add a little extra olive oil to the skillet, if you need to, and brown the chicken pieces on all sides. This will take about 20 minutes. Remove the browned chicken to a plate.

Add the chicken stock (not the saffron-infused stock) to the skillet with the sherry and scrape up the sediment with a wooden spoon to deglaze the pan. Let the liquids bubble together for a few minutes, then return the chicken to the skillet. Add the bay and thyme leaves, crushing them between your fingers. Cover with the lid and simmer for another 10 minutes.

Grind the toasted almonds in a blender or food processor until they reach the coarse side of ground. Tear the fried bread into pieces and add to the nuts with the fried garlic, parsley, and saffron-infused chicken stock. Process to a puree.

Scrape this mixture into the chicken pan and stir to amalgamate with the juices. If it looks very thick, add a little more hot chicken stock. Taste and adjust the seasoning and add a spritz of lemon juice. Taste again—you may need a little more lemon juice—then serve.

I cut the chicken legs and breasts in half to give 8 pieces, saving the wings for another dish (page 10), or to make stock along with the carcass (page 14).

Grilled broccoli with Romesco

Romesco sauce is great with firm-fleshed white fish or a Spanish tortilla (page 169). It is also good with grilled broccoli. (Here, broccolini has been grilled.) It gives oomph to anything that needs a strong, hot partner to jazz it up a little. You may make it with just almonds or hazelnuts, if that's all you have.

If you don't have a griddle, I'm afraid you won't achieve the grilled flavor, but you can finish the broccoli after blanching it by roasting it in a hot oven with the oil, chile, and garlic. Still good, just different.

Serves 4.

2 heads of broccoli, broken into florets, or ¾ to 1 pound broccolini

3 to 4 tablespoons good, fruity olive oil

1 green chile, minced, or 1 teaspoon dried red chile flakes

1 garlic clove, peeled and sliced

coarse salt and black pepper

for the Romesco

¼ cup (scant) blanched Marcona almonds

4 tablespoons good, fruity olive oil

2 garlic cloves, peeled and minced

1 thick slice stale, good brown or white bread, crusts removed

1 cup canned plum or diced tomatoes

1 red chile, seeded and minced, or ¼ to ½ teaspoon cayenne pepper to taste

¼ cup (scant) whole roasted hazelnuts

2 tablespoons red wine vinegar

¼ cup fino sherry

First make the Romesco. Preheat the oven to 300 degrees F. Scatter the almonds on a small baking dish and toast in the oven for 5 to 10 minutes until golden, keeping a close eye on them, as they will color quickly.

Slowly heat 2 tablespoons olive oil in a pan with the minced garlic; when hot, remove the garlic with a slotted spoon and reserve. Sauté the bread briefly on both sides in the garlicky oil until crisp and brown, then remove to the garlic plate.

Add another 2 tablespoons olive oil to the pan and add the tomatoes with the chopped chile or cayenne (start with ¼ teaspoon and add more if needed). Cook down until as thick as jam, about 20 minutes. Remove from the heat and set aside to cool.

Grind the hazelnuts and almonds together in a food processor. Tear the bread into chunks and add to the processor with the sautéed garlic, wine vinegar, and sherry. Blend together. Add the cooled tomato sauce and blend to a coarse paste.

To cook the broccoli, throw the florets into a large pan of rapidly boiling, salted water and blanch for 2 minutes. Immediately drain in a colander and refresh with cold water to arrest the cooking process and retain the color. Drain well.

Heat up the griddle. Dry the broccoli florets with paper towels, then put them into a bowl. Pour over 2 tablespoons olive oil and toss with your hands to coat the florets, then sprinkle with the chile.

When the griddle is really hot, lay the florets on it, leaving room in between to use the tongs. Turn them once they have scorch marks. Spike the stalks with a skewer to check when they are tender.

Meanwhile, heat another 1 or 2 tablespoons olive oil very slowly in a small pan with the garlic. Remove from the heat the moment it is hot.

Place the broccoli in a serving bowl, pour the warm garlicky oil over, and season. Serve at once with the Romesco sauce.

Provençal bread crumbs

Store these bread crumbs in an airtight container and you'll have a lovely gratin top at your fingertips for stuffed baked zucchini, eggplant, bell peppers, or tomatoes, or for sprinkling over prosciutto-wrapped leeks, asparagus, or fennel baked in a béchamel sauce, scattering grated Parmesan over the crumbs before baking or broiling. You can also keep these herbed crumbs in the freezer in a Ziploc bag and sprinkle them over things while still frozen.

I add Parmesan, Gruyère, and Cheddar to Provençal bread crumbs to top macaroni and cheese, or just Parmesan to the crumbs to finish a baked pasta dish.

Or you can mix finely chopped olives and anchovies into the herbed crumbs, fry them all together in extra olive oil and butter, and toss them into pasta with some crème fraîche and dried tomatoes (page 161) for supper. A dry chile crumbled in peps up the heat.

You may just want to fry the herbed crumbs in olive oil and scatter them over broccoli or cauliflower or brussels sprouts, if you are serving game.

3 average-size slices stale, good brown or white bread

a bunch of flat-leaf parsley

4 sprigs of thyme

4 sprigs of savory

1 sprig of rosemary

2 or 3 garlic cloves, peeled and roughly chopped

2 tablespoons good olive oil

coarse salt and black pepper

Preheat the oven to 300 degrees F. Lay the bread slices out on a large baking sheet and place in the oven for 5 to 10 minutes to dry out. Tear the dry bread into chunks.

Strip all the herb leaves from their stems and place them in a food processor with the garlic. Process to chop the herbs finely. Throw in the bread and blend to a coarse crumb texture. Place in a bowl.

Add the olive oil and seasoning, toss to coat, and store in a bag or an airtight container.

Crumbs to coat fish

Blend a good handful of basil leaves with 2 garlic cloves and ¼ cup fruity olive oil in a food processor, then mix with about ¾ cup dry stale bread crumbs, the grated zest and juice of a lemon, 2 skinned, seeded, minced large tomatoes, and some salt and pepper.

You may either coat egged fillets of flounder or other white fish with this or spread a little on top of steamed mussels or clams sitting on their half shells and then broil them until browned and sizzling.

Spaghetti with broccoli,
chile, and fried bread crumbs

Pasta and bread crumbs may not immediately seem appealing, but "cucina povera" (peasant food) is a fact of life in Italy, whether you are impoverished or rich. In poorer regions, such as Puglia and much of southern Italy, people eat the same food whatever their income, which says a lot about both the people and the food, and all to the good. If you can't afford Parmesan, pecorino, or meat, your pasta can still be dressed in its best with sautéed bread crumbs and a few flavorings. You may or may not wish to add a little anchovy and some pine nuts.

Serves 4.

1 pound broccoli

1 pound whole-wheat or ordinary spaghetti

salt

4 to 5 tablespoons best olive oil

3 garlic cloves, peeled and thinly sliced

2 teaspoons dried chile flakes or 1 dried Kashmiri chile, crumbled

1 thick slice stale, good brown or white bread, crusts removed, blended to crumbs

4 anchovies, minced (optional)

¼ cup pine nuts (optional)

Trim the broccoli and break into florets as necessary. I also use the parts of the stalk that aren't tough, peeling and slicing them into disks.

Add the spaghetti to a pot of well-salted boiling water and cook until *al dente*.

Meanwhile, very gently warm 2 tablespoons olive oil in a large skillet with the sliced garlic and chile.

In another skillet, heat 2 to 3 tablespoons olive oil. When hot, throw in the bread crumbs and stir to coat. Turn the heat down and keep shifting the crumbs around in the pan until they are golden and crunchy; they must not darken.

In the meantime, throw the broccoli into a pot of fast-boiling water and cook for 3 minutes or until just tender.

Add the anchovies and pine nuts to the garlic and chile pan, if you are using them. Drain the broccoli, refresh under cold water, and throw into the pan, too, stirring to mix with the other ingredients. You may need a little more oil at this stage.

Drain the pasta, retaining a little water and pour it into the garlic, chile, and broccoli. Toss to combine, then throw in the crumbs and turn to coat. Serve from the pan.

Rhubarb brioche and butter pudding

There are few things more keenly worked and reinvented than the great bread and butter pudding. My allegiance to brioche and butter pudding with an apricot glaze, bread and butter pudding with prunes and dried apricots, and chocolate bread and butter pudding must now expand for a fourth contender in the best-of-the-best stakes. Here it is. You may make it with croissants or with bread if you prefer. It is the rhubarb and ginger that give the heart-stopping creamy, eggy butteriness a shock of sharpness—cutting the richness with fruit and spice perfectly.

My 12-year-old friend Izzy, a keen cook who lives in the village, helped me make this when I dreamed it up, and I promised, in return, that she would get a mention if the pudding were good enough for this book.

Serves 8.

for the fruit layer

2¼ pounds rhubarb, trimmed and cut into short lengths

¾ cup (rounded) unrefined granulated sugar

finely grated zest and juice of 1 orange

1 ball stem ginger preserved in syrup, finely diced, plus 3 tablespoons syrup from the jar

for the custard layer

1¼ cups whole milk

1¼ cups heavy cream

1 vanilla bean, split, seeds scraped out

3 organic large eggs

½ cup superfine vanilla sugar

for the bread layer

4 high-quality brioches or all-butter croissants

Preheat the oven to 350 degrees F. Put the rhubarb into a wide, shallow, heavy-bottomed pan. Scatter the sugar, orange zest, and juice over, and add the ginger with its syrup. Place over medium heat and move the rhubarb around carefully, so as not to break it up. Cook until the sugar has dissolved and the fruit is at the stage where it is a little squishy but still retaining its shape. Remove the rhubarb to a sieve and allow the juice to drip into a bowl beneath; save the juice for the glaze.

For the custard, pour the milk and cream into a heavy-bottomed pan and add the vanilla seeds and bean. Heat slowly, removing the pan from the heat before the liquid boils. Meanwhile, whisk the eggs and sugar together in a bowl. Strain the infused milk and pour onto the egg mixture, whisking well.

Split the brioches or croissants in half horizontally. Place the bottom halves in a single layer in a greased baking dish and plop the rhubarb evenly over the surface. Arrange the brioche or croissant top halves over the rhubarb and pour the custard mixture evenly over the top.

Stand the baking dish in a large roasting pan and pour in enough boiling water to come halfway up the sides of the baking dish. Bake in the middle of the oven for 40 to 50 minutes until the custard is set through. A faint wobble in the middle is fine, as the dish will continue cooking as it cools.

Leave the pudding in the bain-marie to keep it warm. Meanwhile, for the glaze, pour the reserved rhubarb syrup into a small pan and bubble over medium heat to reduce by half until thick and jammy. Brush this over the top of the pudding to give a luscious pink glaze. Serve hot or warm, with cream, if desired.

Baked peach brown Betty

I love the lightness of a Betty when a crumble seems too heavy—in this case a lovely roasted peach with the crunch of buttery crumb and amaretti. The end result is definitely a whole fruit, not a purée or a compote. You can also make it using nectarines, plums, greengages, or apricots. If you do not have any amaretti or similar Italian cookies, use extra crumbs and add a little natural almond extract with the sugar.

Serves 6.

6 medium or 3 large ripe peaches, ideally white

1½ cups brown bread crumbs

juice of ½ lemon (if peeling the peaches)

4 tablespoons light muscovado sugar or light brown sugar

½ cup dessert wine, Pedro Ximénez, or oloroso sherry

6 amaretti cookies

4 tablespoons (½ stick) unsalted butter

Preheat the oven to 350 degrees F. Choose an au gratin dish or heavy-bottomed ovenproof pan that will hold the peaches, once halved, snugly. Scatter the bread crumbs on a baking sheet and toast in the oven for 5 minutes or until dry.

If you prefer to skin the peaches, steep them in a bowl of boiling hot water for a minute, then remove and peel away the skins. Halve and pit the fruit and rub the cut surfaces with a little lemon juice. Put the peach halves cut-side-up in the baking dish and sprinkle with 1 tablespoon of the muscovado (or brown) sugar. Pour the wine or sherry around them.

Crush the amaretti into the toasted bread crumbs, add the remaining sugar, and mix well. Sprinkle a layer of the crumb mixture over the peach halves and dot with butter. Bake for 30 minutes or until the peaches are cooked and the topping is bubbling and brown.

Serve with plenty of whipped cream, into which you might like to whisk 1 or 2 tablespoons pêche de vigne liqueur, if you have some.

Pain perdu with fruit compote

In medieval times this lovely, simple dish was eaten in both England and France. It was originally made from bread baked with the finest flour, which was dipped in beaten egg before frying, spicing, and sugaring. It really is as good for breakfast or brunch as it is for dessert.

For the compote, I love to combine strawberries and rhubarb when strawberries are in season. A mix of blueberries, strawberries, and raspberries is also delicious: toss in half the amount of sugar suggested for the rhubarb and briefly warm in a pan—just to get the juices flowing.

Serves 4.

4 slices good day-old bread, crusts removed if preferred

¼ cup light cream

3 organic large eggs

1 tablespoon sherry or Madeira

1½ tablespoons unsalted butter

1 to 2 teaspoons superfine vanilla sugar

½ teaspoon ground cinnamon, ideally freshly ground

for the compote

1 pound rhubarb, cut into short lengths on the diagonal

4 tablespoons light muscovado or unrefined granulated sugar

1¾ cups halved strawberries

Cut each slice of bread into two triangles. Whisk the cream, eggs, and sherry or Madeira together in a bowl.

Now start the compote: put the rhubarb into a heavy-bottomed skillet and scatter the sugar over the fruit. Cook over moderate heat until just tender but still holding its shape, turning from time to time—carefully, so as not to break up the fruit.

Meanwhile, melt the butter in a skillet until foaming but not brown. Dunk each slice of bread in the creamy mixture, turning to soak both sides. Slip the triangles of dunked bread into the skillet and fry on both sides until golden brown and crisp.

When the rhubarb is almost ready, toss in the strawberries and heat through for a couple of minutes.

Lay the pain perdu in a warmed serving dish and sprinkle lightly with a little superfine vanilla sugar mixed with cinnamon. Serve with the fruit compote.

Summer pudding

To my mind, nothing speaks more obviously of summer, abundance, and sheer fruitiness than a summer pudding. Here I am not reinventing the wheel, I'm just using less bread and defining the fruits more clearly by cooking them separately. Raspberries and blackberries are classic partners, though strawberries can be part of the equation, too. Cherries and red currants, in their short seasons, are lovely additions, while blueberries are a year-round alternative. Of course, you can make individual puddings, if you prefer. The pudding needs to be made a day ahead and refrigerated overnight.

Serves 6 to 8.

a day-old loaf of good white bread, sliced and crusts removed

1 pound raspberries

½ cup superfine vanilla sugar

2 cups strawberries, sliced

1 tablespoon kirsch

1½ cups (rounded) blackberries

2 tablespoons crème de cassis

1½ cups blueberries, or use red currants or pitted cherries in season

spritz of lemon juice

unrefined confectioners' sugar, to taste

Preheat the oven to 300 degrees F. Lay the bread slices on a large baking sheet and place in the oven for 5 to 10 minutes to dry out.

Set aside a third of the raspberries for the sauce. Throw the rest into a wide, heavy-bottomed pan, sprinkle with 1 tablespoon sugar and heat gently until the fruit just starts to bleed but does not lose its shape. Instantly place in a bowl. Repeat with all of the strawberries, adding 1 tablespoon kirsch and scattering a scant tablespoon of sugar over them. Next the blackberries, with 1 tablespoon cassis and a heaping tablespoon of sugar, and finally the blueberries with 1 tablespoon sugar and 1 tablespoon cassis again, to bring out their flavor.

Cut a circle of bread to fit the bottom of a 1¼-quart capacity bowl and press into place. Spoon a layer of fruit and juice on top. Add another bread circle and a different layer of fruit, then repeat two or three times to fill the bowl. You need room for a final layer of bread.

Put a saucer or plate on top of the pudding—one that just fits inside the bowl—and place some heavy weights on top. Refrigerate overnight.

The next day, for the sauce, process the reserved raspberries in a blender, then sieve and add a spritz of lemon and confectioners' sugar to taste. Turn the pudding out onto a plate and pour the raspberry sauce over. Serve with whipped cream.

Supper for a song

I feel that I have sung for my supper all my life, although I was pretty scratchy and out of tune when I started, in fact I simply didn't have a clue.

It all began at university, where the food was really so bad that I decided to teach myself to cook. I had to invent "supper for a song" every night, and in the absence of money I had to make do. To begin with, I didn't know whether I had even a modicum of talent for cooking; and whatever I might have was, as yet, unharnessed to any skills or knowledge. But I had greed, an appetite for good food, and an appetite to learn how to cook, which remain undimmed. I didn't see the desire to cook a good dinner as an inferior pastime, as some of my fellow students did. I guess I didn't realize back then that I was setting out on a way of life in which good food would always play a vital role.

I started cooking every night, and slowly the triumphs began to overtake the disasters, and my growing confidence and technique turned budding love to burning obsession. Food is my passion—well, one of them—and continues to be, thirty years since I cooked my first dinner. Cooking became part of the fabric of my life, and then my life; I could never not sing for my supper. I still take the greatest pride in inventing suppers for a song—the most creative and satisfying way of cooking.

And always with a song. Music and cooking are mighty fine accompaniments. I simply have no idea how Saturday afternoons would pass without cooking to the BBC's "Jazz Record Requests," any more than the evenings would begin in earnest without the

dulcet tones of Sean Rafferty on his classical program "In Tune."
When my son Harry is at home I have my very own resident
minstrel, plus guitar, for which I'm happy to offer the ultimate
reward, supper for a song.

Cooking a good supper is the best way to win friends and
influence and disarm enemies. Getting people to talk around a
kitchen table is one thing; give them food and friendship follows.
Well, that's what I've found ever since my fledgling attempts at
nineteen in an ill-equipped kitchen with the most basic ingredients,
a few simple recipes, and a group of starving students.

If the purse strings are tight, but you have imagination,
passion, and a dedication to the table, you can cook a good dinner.
And cooking for friends around you, whatever your budget—you
can always ask them to contribute—is part of the same idea, part
of the great communal feast of life, which isn't about extravagance
and showing off; it's about good food and good company.

Here are some of my favorite dishes and dinners. Sometimes
the luxury of something special like fine wild salmon might not
appear, at first glance, to be part of the supper-for-a-song hymn
sheet; but look a little closer, see how all the surrounding
ingredients and accompanying dishes are chosen to minimize the
one extravagance—something we can all do with a little thought.

Have a bit of a splurge one day, cook a something-out-of-nothing
supper (pages 164–185) the next. Don't make false or misery-
inducing economies. Great taste foremost, uppermost—not just
most, but all of the time. Let the gastronomic aria commence.

Crushed peas with feta and scallions

This is a lovely dish to serve with grilled pita bread, either alongside a couple of other mezze, while you have a drink before supper, or as an appetizer in its own right, or as a light lunch with a good salad on the side. In the summer, please use fresh peas; at all other times of year the wondrous frozen pea will do. You can make this dish in advance, put it in the fridge, and bring it back to room temperature when you want it.

Serves 4 to 6 as an appetizer.

2¼ pounds peas in the pod, or 1½ cups frozen organic peas or petit pois

2 to 4 tablespoons fruity olive oil

½ pound sheep's-milk feta, drained

½ pound Greek-style yogurt

1 garlic clove, peeled and minced with a little coarse salt

a bunch of scallions, trimmed and finely sliced

a large handful of mint leaves, shredded

juice of 1 lemon

coarse salt and black pepper

If using fresh peas, shell them and cook briefly in boiling water until *al dente*, then drain well and place in a large bowl. Sprinkle with 2 tablespoons olive oil and crush them coarsely with a potato masher.

If you are using frozen peas, blanch them briefly, drain exceptionally well, and crush before adding the oil, pouring off any more excess water at this stage; add the oil bit by bit and less liberally.

Mash the feta and yogurt together in a shallow bowl. While the peas are still hot, add the feta and toss to combine. This is all about texture, not smoothness, as for a dip. Add the minced garlic.

Now add the scallions and 2 tablespoons shredded mint. Stir in the juice of half a lemon to start with. Season with pepper and a little salt, if you think it is needed; feta is pretty salty. Taste and adjust the seasoning, adding more lemon juice, mint, or olive oil if you like.

Serve in a shallow dish with a mound of warm, grilled pita bread.

Pea, mint, and scallop custards

Years ago the brilliant chef Rowley Leigh, now at Le Café Anglais, in London, then at Kensington Place, came up with a delectable dish of scallops served on a minted pea puree. It was one of those elegantly simple, understated things that owed everything to the understanding of restraint, of not going a flavor too far.

But it is another dish I have been cooking for years, a crab custard, that led me to wonder about making a creamy, crushed pea and mint custard, concealing scallops and their hectically colored roe beneath, until you hit the last mouthful. It worked a treat. Adding the white of the scallop whole and raw, the roe likewise, caused them to poach perfectly without overcooking. Two small scallops, or one large one, per ramekin is hardly the price of a mortgage. If you can't find scallops with roe then you can, of course, omit them. This dish is one I will make and make.

12 medium or 6 large
scallops, cleaned

3 tablespoons unsalted
butter

4 tablespoons heavy cream

1¾ cups frozen organic
petit pois

2 organic large eggs, beaten,
plus 3 extra yolks

8 to 10 mint leaves, minced

coarse salt and black pepper

Preheat the oven to 350 degrees F. Separate the roe, if attached, from the scallop disks, keeping them whole; set both aside.

Melt the butter in a pan, add 3 tablespoons of the cream, and heat to scalding point. Now add the peas and stir them until they are just cooked through, about 5 minutes.

Remove from the heat and add the last of the cream. Beat in the egg yolks, one by one, followed by the beaten eggs. Stir in about three-quarters of the mint and some seasoning.

Scrape the mixture into a blender and blend so briefly that you can barely count to 3. The whole point is to keep the peas rough textured, not smooth. Taste again, and if you need to, add the last of the mint, which should scent but not intrude.

Boil a kettle of water. Meanwhile, plop one or two white scallops and their roe, if using, into the bottom of each of 6 ramekins. Spoon the pea mixture over the top. Stand the ramekins in a roasting pan and pour in enough boiling water to come halfway up their sides. Lay an oiled piece of waxed paper over the top to stop a skin from forming on the custards.

Cook in the center of the oven for 20 minutes. Give the roasting pan a little shake to check the custards. They should have set; if not, give them another 5 minutes.

Remove the ramekins from the roasting pan and place each one on a small plate. Serve warm.

Spiced chicken liver mousse with blackened onions

This dish is inspired by my favorite appetizer at The Malabar, an Indian restaurant in Notting Hill—fried whole chicken livers coated in blackened onions, which arrives on a sizzling karahi (India's answer to the wok). The soft meat, with the spiced, crunchy onion is divine.

These little spicy ramekins of liver are as smooth as silk, with a hint of fennel seed, coriander, and cumin. I serve them with grilled spice-coated onions and fingers of toast. The mousse is rich, so a small ramekin is really enough. Serve warm or cold.

Serves 6 to 8 as an appetizer.

1¾ pounds organic chicken livers, trimmed of all sinew

a little milk to soak

1½ teaspoons fennel seeds

1 teaspoon cumin seeds

1 teaspoon coriander seeds

½ teaspoon cayenne pepper

2 organic large eggs, plus 3 extra yolks

1 cup heavy cream

⅔ cup (scant) milk

3 tablespoons plus 1 teaspoon butter, melted and cooled to tepid

coarse salt and black pepper

for the blackened onions

1 large onion, peeled and sliced

a little olive oil to coat

½ teaspoon dried chile flakes

1½ teaspoons nigella (black onion) seeds

1 teaspoon ground turmeric

1½ teaspoons toasted cumin seeds

to serve

a small handful of cilantro leaves, chopped (optional)

toast fingers

Put the chicken livers into a bowl, pour on enough milk to cover, and leave to soak for an hour or so. Preheat the oven to 300 degrees F. Lightly grease 6 to 8 small ramekins with butter.

Pour off the milk from the chicken livers and dry them on paper towels. Toast the fennel and cumin seeds gently for about a minute in a dry pan until they start to release their fragrance; don't let them over-brown. Tip into a mortar and crush, together with the coriander seeds.

Put the chicken livers into a blender and add the crushed spices, cayenne, eggs and extra yolks, cream, milk, and melted butter. Season. Blend for about 5 minutes—longer than seems sane. Using a wooden spoon, push the mixture through a sieve into a bowl.

Boil a kettle of water. Divide the mixture between the ramekins. Stand them in a roasting pan and pour in enough boiling water to come halfway up their sides. Lay a sheet of greased waxed paper on top and cook in the middle of the oven for 35 minutes.

Meanwhile, for the blackened onions, toss the sliced onion in a bowl with a little olive oil, then add the spices and some seasoning and turn to coat. Heat a griddle, or a heavy-bottomed pan, if you don't have one. When it is really hot, throw on the onion slices and cook until they have browned and charred in places. They will not soften quite enough on the griddle, so transfer them to a heated skillet to finish cooking, adding a little more oil if they begin to stick. Taste and adjust the spicing and seasoning.

When the mousses are cooked, remove from the oven and leave to stand in the bain-marie for 10 minutes.

To turn out, run a small, sharp knife around the edge of each mousse and invert onto a plate. Put a little heap of blackened onions next to each one and scatter a little chopped cilantro over the plate, if you like. Serve with hot toast.

Pickled mackerel and potato salad

This refreshing, vibrant dish is great to start a supper with. Get pickling the night before you want to eat it, and get the fish seller to skin and fillet the mackerel, which must be spanking fresh.

Serves 6 as an appetizer.

3 mackerel, skinned and filleted, pin bones removed

for the marinade

½ cup olive oil

½ cup dry white wine

¼ cup white wine vinegar

2 tablespoons Pernod

1 organic lemon, thinly sliced

2 bay leaves

2 sprigs each of parsley, dill, and thyme

1 carrot, peeled and thinly sliced

1 celery stalk, strings removed with a potato peeler and thinly sliced

1 shallot or small red onion, peeled and thinly sliced

1 level tablespoon muscovado sugar or brown sugar

pinch of coarse salt

6 white peppercorns

chopped dill or chives to serve (optional)

for the potato salad

1 pound waxy salad potatoes, such as Yellow Finn

1 shallot, peeled and minced

4 tablespoons olive oil, or more

1 tablespoon white wine or tarragon vinegar

2 tablespoons chopped flat-leaf parsley

coarse salt and black pepper

Check the mackerel fillets for any pin bones, then cut into strips, about 1½" long and ½" wide. Mix all the marinade ingredients together in a sealable glass or plastic container, and add the mackerel strips. Make sure they are submerged in the marinade, seal the container, and refrigerate for 12 to 18 hours.

A couple of hours before you want to eat it, make the salad. Boil the potatoes until just tender, then drain and slice them while hot. Toss into a bowl and mix with all the other salad ingredients. Check the seasoning and set aside until ready to serve. You may need to add a little more olive oil later, as the potatoes absorb a lot, and you may need to sharpen them up with a little more vinegar.

When ready to serve, place a generous spoonful of potato salad on each plate and top with strips of marinated mackerel and the marinade vegetables. You may wish to sprinkle a little chopped dill or chives over the salad.

Carrot, apple, and blue cheese soup

I think I must have been thinking ploughman's lunch in a bowl for this, but the combination of sweet carrot, sharp apple, and salty cheese works brilliantly.

When I am making soups, I regularly use water if I haven't any stock on hand and look for something else to create body. More often than not, I will find a strong, vibrant ingredient to do this, lending depth and clarity. The three main ingredients in this soup all play a role in defining its character.

Serves 4 as appetizer.

2 to 3 tablespoons olive oil

1 small red or white onion, peeled and minced

1 garlic clove, peeled and minced

coarse salt and black pepper

1 large organic carrot, peeled and minced

1 large cooking apple

1 quart water

2 to 3 ounces good blue cheese, such as Stilton or Roquefort

Warm the olive oil in a large, heavy-bottomed pot and sauté the onion and garlic, with a sprinkle of salt to help the onion juices run, over medium heat for a few minutes. Add the carrot, stir to coat in the oil, and cook for about 10 minutes until it is beginning to soften.

Meanwhile, peel, quarter, and core the apple and cut into slices. Add to the pot and cook together for a couple of minutes.

Add the water, a ladleful at a time, so that it heats up more quickly. Bring to a simmer, put the lid on, and continue to simmer for 10 minutes. Remove from the heat and season with pepper only.

Liquidize the soup in a blender in batches as necessary, crumbling in the blue cheese as you do so. Taste critically. You may need a little more cheese, or you may need to adjust the seasoning.

Return the soup to the pot and bring to a simmer again before serving.

Middle Eastern stuffed peppers

I don't quite know how stuffed bell peppers got a bad name and became something of a joke. It must have been because of horribly stuffed, semi-raw peppers, filled with dried-up rice and greasy ground meat. In reality, a well-stuffed pepper is a beauty to behold and to eat—and just as good cold the next day. This is how I cooked mine in Ireland this summer, and I'm still not sure whether hot, warm, or cold gets the prize; they were all lovely.

If there are two of you, keep 4 stuffed pepper halves for another meal. Cool, then refrigerate, bringing them up to room temperature an hour before you want to eat them cold. They will need a little more olive oil sprinkled over them the following day and perhaps some freshly chopped parsley and/or mint and a little more toasted cumin.

Serves 4.

4 bell peppers, red and yellow, or all red

for the stuffing

1 cup brown basmati rice

½ cinnamon stick

4 cardamom pods

about 5 tablespoons olive oil

1 medium onion, peeled and minced

1 carrot, peeled and diced

2 garlic cloves, peeled and sliced

1 zucchini, trimmed and cut into small dice

½ teaspoon cayenne pepper, or to taste

1 teaspoon ground ginger

2 to 3 tablespoons leftover tomato sauce of any kind (page 174), or canned organic diced tomatoes in juice

2 tablespoons pine nuts, toasted in the oven or in a dry skillet

a handful of raisins, soaked in warm water for 30 minutes and drained

a small bunch of cilantro, leaves stripped and chopped

coarse salt and black pepper

3 to 4 ladlefuls chicken stock

chopped parsley or mint, to finish (optional)

Preheat the oven to 400 degrees F. Cut the peppers in half vertically through their stalks and remove their seeds and white membranes. Place cut side up in a baking dish.

Cook the rice, according to the instructions on the package, with the cinnamon and cardamom, until *al dente*.

Meanwhile, heat 2 tablespoons olive oil in a large, heavy-bottomed skillet, then add the minced onion and carrot, turning them to coat. Cook over medium heat for about 5 minutes, then add the garlic and zucchini, with the cayenne and ginger. Keep stirring for a few minutes until everything is turning translucent and softening.

Add your leftover tomato sauce or canned tomatoes in juice at this point, stirring them in. Cook for another 5 minutes or so, then take off the heat and add the toasted pine nuts, drained raisins, chopped cilantro, and seasoning.

When the rice is ready, drain it well and discard the spices. Add enough of the cooked rice to the vegetable mixture to ensure a well-balanced stuffing that doesn't err on the side of too much basmati. (You can keep any leftover rice to dress up as a spiced rice salad and eat cold.) Add a little of the chicken stock to the mixture to lubricate the rice; again, use your judgment.

Spoon the mixture into the pepper halves in the baking dish, piling it up generously. Add a few ladlefuls of stock to the dish and drizzle some olive oil over each pepper half.

Cover the top of the roasting pan with a sheet of oiled waxed paper to prevent the rice from drying out. Bake for 40 to 45 minutes, checking the peppers after 20 minutes or so, as you may need to add a little more stock to the roasting pan.

Serve the peppers hot, warm, or cold, scattered with chopped parsley or mint, if you like.

Stuffed calamari

The stuffing for the Middle Eastern peppers on the previous page is every bit as good in calamari (aka squid) pouches, gently poached in red wine. The thing about calamari is that there's no middle way. Cook it short and hot or cook it long and slow and you have meaty tenderness. Anything else and you may as well chew a blanket. Red wine and black ink, the little frilly bits, and the stuffed, giant pockets submerged beneath the vino make this a lovely dish to serve with an extra green vegetable on the side. And calamari are still among the cheapest seafood you can buy—a fish for our financial times.

Serves 2.

2 medium calamari, about ½ pound each

about ⅓ quantity rice stuffing (from Middle Eastern peppers, page 133)

a handful of peas and/or skinned fava beans

coarse salt and black pepper

about 1½ cups red wine

a little good olive oil (optional)

a handful of flat-leaf parsley, chopped (optional)

Preheat the oven to 300 degrees F. Clean the calamari by pulling the tentacles and head from the body. Cut off the tentacles and discard the head. Remove the transparent quill from the body pouch—also the soft, gooey bits. Keep the ink sacs (or you can buy a sachet of squid ink from the fish seller if your calamari is already cleaned). Rinse the body pouches and tentacles.

Have the stuffing ready. Stir the peas and/or fava beans into the mixture and check the seasoning. Stuff the pouches three-quarters full with the mixture—no more or they will burst. Lay them next to each other snugly in a baking dish and add the tentacles.

Heat the red wine in a pan, then pour enough into the baking dish to come halfway up the sides of the stuffed calamari. Add the calamari ink. Cover the dish with foil and braise in the oven for 2½ hours, turning the calamari over halfway through the cooking time. Insert a skewer into the calamari to check that it is tender; it may need another 30 minutes. The white calamari flesh colors a lovely rusty garnet in the inky wine.

Leave to stand for 10 minutes out of the oven. You may like to add a libation of olive oil and a scattering of parsley before serving.

Wild salmon
with smoked eggplant polenta and hot cucumber

It is not just that I am driven by the seasons, it is that I could not contemplate eating farmed salmon. Beg to differ if you will, but I would rather have one fine Irish salmon from the Bundorragha or the Bunowen rivers in County Mayo in the summer than eat farmed salmon steaks throughout the year. Wild Alaskan salmon doesn't have quite the flavor of my Atlantic heroes, but it is in such a different league from the farmed that I can only urge you to experiment.

Here the quality of real polenta with the subterfuge, smoky surprise of the eggplant and the pale green still-crisp cucumber, both a steal, offset any perceived extravagance. Seek out proper polenta. Made with cornmeal, it is the color of egg yolk and far superior to quick-cook polenta, which has no discernible flavor.

The colors are exquisite in this dish, though quite how I came upon the unusual combination I cannot recall. It is pure heaven, I assure you, and needs no extras.

Serves 4.

4 wild salmon fillets
1 tablespoon unsalted butter
coarse salt and black pepper

for the polenta

2½ to 3 cups coarse-grain
yellow polenta, depending on
appetite
2 quarts water
2 to 3 teaspoons salt
1 eggplant
1½ tablespoons butter

for the cucumber

2 small to medium
cucumbers
2 teaspoons unsalted butter
about ⅔ cup heavy cream
2 heaping teaspoons chopped
tarragon

For the polenta, bring the water to a boil in a large, wide, heavy-bottomed pot. Add 2 to 3 teaspoons salt. Pour in the polenta slowly, in a steady stream, stirring with a whisk until smooth. At this stage, over high heat, the mixture will splutter and jump out of the pot, so wrap a cloth around your hand and stir with a long-handled wooden spoon. After 5 minutes you may turn the heat down and stir less regularly over the next 40 to 50 minutes.

In the meantime, prick the eggplant in a few places with the tip of a knife. Hold it with a pair of tongs over a charcoal grill or gas flame and char it thoroughly on all sides. It should cook through in 5 minutes or so, but test with a skewer. Alternatively, you can roast the eggplant in the oven at 375 degrees F until tender, although you will not attain the smokiness.

Remove the cooked eggplant to a bowl, cover with plastic wrap, and leave until you can handle it, then peel away all the charred skin. Put the luscious flesh into a bowl and mash it coarsely with a fork.

Peel the cucumbers and halve them lengthwise, then scoop the seeds out with a small teaspoon. Cut into short lengths.

About 5 minutes before the polenta is likely to be ready, you should start to cook the fish and cucumber.

To cook the cucumber, melt the butter in a pan and add the cucumber with a pinch of salt. Cook for a couple of minutes, then add the cream and tarragon and continue to cook until the sauce thickens and the cucumber is still crisp, yet not resistant. Check the seasoning and remove from the heat.

At the same time, to cook the fish, heat the butter in a heavy-bottomed skillet. Season the salmon fillets and place them skin side down in the bubbling butter. Cook over medium heat until you can see that the flesh has turned a pale pink color halfway up the thickness. Turn over and repeat, but leave a slim stripe of flamingo-bright flesh when you remove the salmon—overcooking fish happens in a whisker.

Keep an eye on the polenta while you cook the fish and cucumber. It will come away from the sides of the pan when it is cooked. At this point, remove it from the heat, add the butter, season, and stir in the mashed eggplant.

Spoon a goodly portion of polenta onto each warmed plate. Perch the salmon on the top and serve a spoonful of cucumber in tarragon cream on the side.

Little fish fillets
with braised fennel and anchovy butter

I make this dish with John Dory, which in the wintertime, when they are small, is very inexpensive. You can substitute flounder or another similar white fish. You need three small fillets per person and they need little more than a brief introduction to the pan. Braised fennel and a simple anchovy butter are ideal accompaniments. A glimmer of green parsley stops this from being an all-white with a-hint-of-pink dish.

Serves 2.

6 small John Dory or flounder fillets, about 7 to 8 ounces fish per person

1 large fennel bulb

a little lemon juice

2 tablespoons olive oil

1 teaspoon finely chopped rosemary needles

½ cup white wine

coarse salt and black pepper

1 tablespoon unsalted butter

1 teaspoon finely minced flat-leaf parsley

for the anchovy butter

4 tablespoons (½ stick) butter, softened to room temperature

3 good-quality anchovies

a little lemon juice

First make the anchovy butter. Put two-thirds of the butter on a small plate and mash in the anchovies until you have a marbled, rather than a uniform pink effect. Add a little spritz of lemon juice and a hint of salt and pepper, then put the butter on a butter paper or piece of waxed paper and roll it into a cylindrical shape, close the paper around it, and freeze for 30 minutes or longer. That way you can cut it from frozen and drop it onto the fish when it's cooked.

Have the fish fillets ready at room temperature. Remove any tough outer leaves from the fennel, then slice the bulb as thin as you possibly can, using a mandoline, if possible. Immediately spritz a little lemon juice over the fennel slices to stop discoloration.

Heat 1 tablespoon olive oil in a skillet, and when hot, add the chopped rosemary. Wait 30 seconds until it fizzles, then add the fennel and stir to coat. Lower the heat so that the fennel cooks down slowly. After a few minutes pour in the wine and let it bubble and begin to reduce. Season. Cook until you have a softened tangle, then transfer to a warm plate with the juice; keep warm.

Add the butter to the pan and heat. When it begins to foam, lay the fish fillets in the pan skin side down and season them. Fry over medium heat for a couple of minutes or until the flesh is translucent halfway up the fillets. Flip them over carefully so that they don't break up and the delicate skin doesn't tear. Cook until opaque, another minute or two, then take off the heat.

Spoon the fennel onto warmed plates and lay the fillets on top. Slice the chilled anchovy butter into disks and place one on top of each fillet. Scatter the parsley over the fish and serve. Green and orange vegetables on the side—to add more color and texture—and mashed potatoes, work well.

Braised chicken and rice
with orange, saffron, almond, and pistachio syrup

Here is a jewel of an Afghani dish. Unusual and exotic, it is one I cook regularly, sometimes with shoulder of lamb instead of chicken thighs. I serve it with slow-cooked spinach, finished with leeks and a minuscule amount of rhubarb. This may sound strange, but the rhubarb is sweetened by the leeks and it really does work.

Serves 4.

1½ cups brown basmati rice

¼ cup olive oil

2 medium onions, peeled and minced

coarse salt and black pepper

4 large chicken thighs, chopped in half, or 8 smaller ones

about 4 cups water

1 large organic orange

1 tablespoon unrefined granulated sugar

½ cup slivered blanched almonds

½ cup shelled, chopped pistachio nuts

large pinch of saffron threads

2 to 3 teaspoons rose water

7 or 8 cardamom pods, lightly crushed, seeds extracted

a handful of blanched, skinned baby fava beans (optional)

a handful of blanched peas (optional)

Rinse the rice in a sieve under cold running water until the water runs clear; put to one side.

Heat the olive oil in a large, heavy-bottomed pot and throw in the onions. Cook over medium heat until they soften and turn golden. Season the chicken thighs and add them to the pan. Brown on all sides, then pour in 2½ cups water and bring to a simmer. Cover with a lid and cook until the chicken is tender, about 20 minutes.

Meanwhile, peel the zest from the orange with a potato peeler, then cut it into matchstick strips. Blanch in a small pan of boiling water for a couple of minutes, then drain.

Dissolve the sugar in ½ cup (scant) water in a small, heavy-bottomed pan over medium heat, then bring to a boil and let bubble to reduce and thicken for 5 to 10 minutes until syrupy. Add the orange zest, slivered almonds, and pistachios and boil for 5 minutes, skimming off any froth. Strain the syrup and return to the pan; set aside the orange zest and nuts. Add the saffron and rose water to the syrup and boil again for 3 minutes, then add the cardamom seeds.

Preheat the oven to 300 degrees F. Strain the stock from the chicken thighs and add the syrup to it. Make this up to 3 cups with more water. Bring it to a boil in an ovenproof casserole and add the rice. Season and add two-thirds of the orange zest and nuts, keeping the rest to one side. Bring back to a boil, then cover and simmer until the rice is cooked. The liquid should have all been absorbed by now.

Bury the chicken and onions in the rice and add the fava beans and peas, if you are including them. Put the lid on and cook in the oven for 20 minutes.

Serve straight from the pan or, if you prefer, in a large, warmed serving dish. Sprinkle the last third of the orange zest and nuts over the top before bringing it to the table.

Stuffed pork fillet with figs and Marsala

This is a simple but beauteous marriage, or rather a double marriage. The four main ingredients—pork, figs, blood sausage, and Marsala—partner and complement each other, without any one of them overwhelming the other. It takes only minutes to flatten, stuff, tie, and brown the pork, the blood sausage deepening the flavor of the meat and stretching it.

When you cut the pork and see the blood sausage encased in white meat—juicy, tender, and sticky with sweet Marsala and figs—you know you have a dish worthy of a dinner party or a special but simple-to-prepare supper.

Please make this with properly reared pork. The fast-bred industrially reared pigs taste how you would expect after such an unpleasant life. The old breeds who have been cavorting and truffling in the mud and had time to lay down a proper coating of fat and flavorsome meat are altogether different.

Serves 4.

1 organic, free-range pork tenderloin (fillet)

leaves from a few sprigs of thyme, chopped

coarse salt and black pepper

1 small or ½ large blood sausage

1 tablespoon olive oil

3 tablespoons butter

1 to 1½ cups Marsala, sweet not dry

4 fresh figs, halved

Preheat the oven to 350 degrees F. Slice down through the middle of the pork tenderloin with a sharp knife to the point at which you can open it out like a book, but it remains in one piece. Sprinkle with a little of the thyme and some coarse salt. Take the sausage out of its skin and crumble it along the middle of the pork fillet, not quite to the ends. Roll up the pork and tie it at intervals with string.

Heat the olive oil and 1½ tablespoons butter in a skillet large enough to hold the pork fillet, until it is foaming. Add the meat and brown on all sides for a few minutes, then remove to a plate and season with salt and pepper.

Pour off any fat that looks brown, then deglaze the pan with 1 cup of Marsala, letting it bubble and reduce by about half. Pour in another cup and reduce a little more, then sprinkle in 1 teaspoon chopped thyme. Stir in the rest of the butter, cut into small pieces, to make the sauce glossy. Add the halved figs and warm for 30 seconds.

Lay the pork fillet in the center of a sheet of waxed paper, large enough to enclose it in a baggy parcel. Plop some figs on top and place the rest alongside. Pour the Marsala sauce over the top. Close the bag by folding up the sides and ends securely and fastening with paper clips. Place on a baking sheet and cook in the oven for 25 minutes.

Let the meat rest *en papillote* for 5 minutes before unwrapping and lifting onto a board. Carve into thick slices and arrange with the figs on a warmed platter or on individual plates. Pour the sauce into a pan and reheat until bubbling, then pour it over the meat. Add a last sprinkle of thyme and serve with mashed potatoes and something green.

Liver and onions
with chile, lime, and fish sauce

Yes, fish sauce. Nothing so odd in Asian or Chinese cooking about marrying shrimp paste or fish sauce with beef or pork, and we traditionally spike anchovy into roast lamb to deepen and underscore the flavor without the effect being at all fishy. That is what this dish is about.

You may make it with lamb's or calf's liver, but the less expensive pig's liver is quite a difficult one to convince people of, and I'm trying to do that here. The pigginess can be overpowering, but not in this case—it's the best dish of liver I've eaten in a long time. The liver came from an organic local breed. Buying a pig by the half or the quarter, with a neighbor or two, is a cost-effective way of getting a properly reared traditional-breed beast of the highest quality.

Serves 2.

1 pound or so pig liver, in 2 thick slices

2 to 3 tablespoons fino sherry

1 tablespoon red wine vinegar

2 large onions, peeled (I used one red, one white)

3 tablespoons olive oil

coarse salt and black pepper

1 teaspoon sugar

1 Kashmiri hot dried chile, crushed, or 1 teaspoon dried chile flakes

1 heaping tablespoon all-purpose flour

1 tablespoon Thai fish sauce

juice of 1 lime

a slug of red wine (whatever you happen to have open)

Put the liver into a shallow dish, pour on the sherry and wine vinegar, and leave to marinate in a cool place for a couple of hours, turning it over several times.

Meanwhile, slice the onions as finely as you possibly can. Heat 1 tablespoon olive oil in a heavy-bottomed pan, add the onions with a little salt, and sweat gently until they wilt. Sprinkle with the sugar and black pepper, cover with the lid, and continue to cook gently, stirring from time to time, for another 20 minutes or so. Remove from the heat.

Drain the liver and dry on both sides with paper towels. On a plate, mix the crushed chile and some salt and pepper with the flour. Heat 2 tablespoons olive oil in a large, heavy-bottomed skillet over brisk heat.

Dip the liver in the chile flour, coating both sides and shaking any excess off, then add to the sizzling oil. Brown for a good 3 minutes if the slices are thick. You will see the cooking process happen, the brown creeping up the red liver as it fries. When it reaches halfway up each slice, flip the liver over and continue to cook for 30 seconds or so.

Add the fish sauce and let it almost bubble away, then pour in the lime juice, followed by the wine. The moment the liver is cooked, remove it to a warm plate; it should still be pink in the middle.

Scrape and deglaze the pan, throw in the cooked onions, and reheat for a minute. Spoon the onions and the juices over the liver and serve with roasted roots and a good helping of mashed potato.

Roasted roots

Preheat oven to 400 degrees F. Peel and slice 1 parsnip and 1 carrot into long, chunky fingers, parboil for 2 to 3 minutes; drain well. Toss in a bowl with 1 diced, peeled medium beet, 1 tablespoon olive oil, 1 tablespoon clear honey, and 1 tablespoon sesame seeds. Heat another 1 tablespoon olive oil in a small roasting tray in the oven. After a few minutes, slosh the vegetables into the hot oil and roast for 25 to 30 minutes until cooked and gooey, turning them to brown all over. Season to taste and serve.

Prune clafoutis

The original clafoutis from Limousin, in France, was made with the region's cherries, but the dish is just as gorgeous in the summer made with raspberries and figs, apricots, or plums.

Midwinter is all about batter puddings, which essentially this is, so I thought I would try making a wintry clafoutis with luscious Agen prunes steeped in an orange liqueur. The final touch to make this extra special was to gratinée it. Serve it with some crème fraîche with a little orange zest and Cointreau whisked in, and it really is heaven.

Serves 6.

for the prunes

2½ cups pitted Agen or California prunes

1 heaping tablespoon vanilla sugar

2 tablespoons Cointreau

butter and sugar for the baking dish, plus a little cinnamon (optional)

for the batter

⅔ cup whole milk

1 heaping tablespoon full-fat crème fraîche

2 tablespoons unsalted butter

2 organic large eggs

¼ cup superfine vanilla sugar, plus extra to gratinée

1 cup (scant) all-purpose flour

Put the prunes into a bowl and sprinkle with the sugar and Cointreau. Leave to soak for 2 to 3 hours, turning every so often.

Preheat the oven to 350 degrees F. Butter a baking dish well, then dust it with sugar mixed with a little cinnamon, if you like, shaking it around until it sticks to the butter.

For the batter, heat the milk and crème fraîche together in a small pan to just below a boil, then remove from the heat and add the butter, stirring to melt it.

Beat the eggs and sugar together, using an electric mixer, until they are pale and have quadrupled in volume, about 5 minutes. Pour in the milk and crème fraîche mixture and fold to combine. Sift in the flour and fold in, whisking out any lumps. The mixture should feel light, frothy, and bubbly to the whisk.

Scatter the prunes in the prepared dish and pour the batter over them. Bake for 30 to 40 minutes or until the batter has clearly set at the outside but is still wobbly in the center.

Heat the broiler. Sprinkle the clafoutis liberally with a layer of sugar and place under the broiler until golden brown.

Serve the clafoutis hot, warm, or at room temperature. I like it with crème fraîche flavored with 1 tablespoon Cointreau and the grated zest of an orange. Plain will do if you prefer.

Fig and raspberry clafoutis

Use 1 pound or so figs, cut in half, and the same amount of raspberries. Heat a good knob of butter in a pan and cook the figs for no more than a minute. Toss in the raspberries and sugar, heat for a few seconds until they bleed, then instantly plop them into the prepared au gratin dish. Make the batter, pour over the fruit, and bake as above. The raspberries will bleed delectably into the batter.

Winter fruit salad

I have long loved bay and citrus. In the winter, when navel oranges arrive—or a little later, when Tarocco oranges from Sicily, and other blood oranges, cast their sunset-colored spell over everything—and there are pomegranates, reminding one of all things bright and exotic, the time comes to make a winter fruit salad that is enough to banish winter blues. This is my current favorite: crimson and green, orange and pink, and not a blue in sight.

Serves 6.

4 navel or blood oranges
2 pink grapefruit
12 to 15 organic Medjool dates
1 pomegranate
6 bay leaves
2 heaping tablespoons unrefined sugar
a handful of pistachio nuts

As you prepare the citrus fruit, save all the juices, tipping them into the heavy-bottomed pan you are going to make the syrup in. Slice the tops and bottoms off 3 oranges and both grapefruit. Work a sharp knife from the top to the bottom of each, removing the peel and white pith together in strips until you have the naked fruit. Trim off all the pithy bits.

Slice the oranges into circles and throw them into the serving bowl. Cut the grapefruit into segments between the membranes and add them to the bowl. Squeeze the remains of the grapefruit over the pan to extract all the juice. Halve and pit the dates and add them to the citrus fruit.

Extract the juice from the remaining orange and add it to the pan. Similarly, squeeze and add the juice from half of the pomegranate; this is difficult but not impossible. Add the bay leaves and sugar to the pan, bring slowly to a boil to dissolve the sugar, and let bubble for a few minutes until you have a syrupy consistency.

At this point, throw in the pistachio nuts, cover the pan with a lid, and leave to cool until warm. The bay will continue to infuse and scent the syrup.

Disgorge the seeds from the remaining pomegranate half into the fruit salad. Pour the warm syrup over the fruit salad, including the bay, which looks pretty but is there purely for decoration.

Cover the fruit salad and put it in the fridge until just before serving. The syrup really is the color of sunset.

Summer berry gratin

Sometimes in the summer, you get berried out. Particularly if you invite people over at the last minute, you want something a little more special than just a bowl of raspberries or strawberries and cream. The great thing about this gratin is that the fruits are not cooked through, so they retain all their intense, raw flavor. And it is splendiferous to present a dish of them under a scorched top of light-as-air sabayon with billows of cream folded into it. The topping can be made in advance and kept in the fridge until the following day, so play it whichever way suits you.

Serves 4.

3 cups (rounded) good-quality strawberries, hulled

3 cups (rounded) raspberries

1 cup blueberries

up to 1 tablespoon unrefined superfine vanilla sugar, to taste

1 to 2 tablespoons crème de cassis or Grand Marnier

for the sabayon

4 organic large egg yolks

½ cup (rounded) unrefined superfine vanilla sugar

juice of 1 lemon

½ cup (scant) heavy cream

Put the berries into a large bowl and scatter the sugar and liqueur over them. Set aside to macerate (see note). After 15 minutes, turn the fruit very gently to encourage the juices to bleed and then leave for another 10 minutes or so.

To make the sabayon, put the egg yolks, sugar, and lemon juice in the top of a double boiler or in a heatproof bowl set over a pan of simmering water, making sure the bowl is not touching the water. Whisk, using a hand-held electric whisk, until the mixture has doubled in volume and thickened to the point at which it will leave a trail on top if you lift the beaters. At this point, remove the top pan or bowl to a worktop, setting it down on a folded dish towel to hold it steady, and continue to whisk until the mixture is cold.

Now whisk the cream to the point at which it has a loose slackness but holds its shape; overwhisking even a little will make it too rigid to incorporate. Fold the cream lightly into the sabayon and either proceed to the finish or, if you are not about to serve the gratin, refrigerate.

Put the macerated fruit into a medium, shallow au gratin dish or divide between heatproof individual shallow serving bowls. Plop the sabayon evenly over the top.

Heat the broiler to its highest setting or get your blowtorch ready. Put the gratin under the broiler for about a minute or wave your blowtorch over the surface until it is golden brown. The burnishing has to happen fast so that the sabayon doesn't separate. Serve at once.

If you are preparing the sabayon in advance, macerate the fruit 30 minutes before gratinéeing to serve.

Caramel and cardamom ice cream with Tarocco oranges

Whoever first dreamed up the pairing of oranges and caramel discovered one of those classic combinations that complement and enhance with such simple grace: the sharp tang of citrus, the bittersweet of burned sugar. This ice cream attains nirvana when served with the sharp bite of the red-fleshed winter Tarocco oranges, from the slopes beneath Etna, in Sicily, or, if you can't find them, with the sweeter, dark red flesh of other blood oranges. You need not use the cardamom if you want to keep the caramel pure, but a whiff of it does work wonders with an orange.

Serves 8.

1 cup (rounded) unrefined superfine vanilla sugar

1 vanilla bean, cut into a few pieces

1½ cups whole milk

8 cardamom pods, gently crushed to open

1¼ cups (scant) heavy cream

8 organic large egg yolks

6 Tarocco or other blood oranges

Slowly heat the sugar with the vanilla bean in a wide, heavy-bottomed skillet without stirring, though if your pan has hot spots you may tilt and swirl it a little, until the sugar has melted completely.

Meanwhile, heat the milk with the cardamom pods to scalding point, then remove from the heat, cover, and leave to infuse for 5 minutes.

Once the sugar has melted, let it brown to a dark mahogany all over, at which point you will see darker bubbles beginning to erupt from beneath. Then, and only then, carefully pour the cream over and stir as the two cohere like molten lava. Remove from the heat.

In the meantime, beat the egg yolks in a bowl, strain the infused milk through a sieve onto them, and whisk together. Whisk the milk and egg mix into the hot caramel as soon as you take it off the heat. Return the pan to gentle heat and stir until it is just below boiling point.

Pour into a heatproof bowl set in a larger bowl full of ice, or just pour into a bowl and cool more slowly, whatever suits your timing. Once cooled, churn in an ice-cream maker until firm. Or freeze in a plastic container, whisking every 30 minutes to break up the ice crystals.

To prepare the oranges, squeeze the juice from two of them and set aside. Cut away the peel and pith from the rest, in strips from top to bottom. Slice the oranges across into circles and place in a dish. Strain the reserved juice over them, then cover and chill until ready to serve.

You'll need only a few orange slices alongside the untold richness of this most tempting of ice creams.

The fruit glut

There's more to this than a bag of frozen fruit. We country mice, with odd fogyish tendencies, are inclined to follow the seasons religiously, disbelieving everything the supermarkets would have us believe about when and how we should buy and eat a peach or cook a salmon. If, like me, you pick, grow, and buy from farmers' markets and bush-fruit growers, watching for the brief season of each fruit, fowl, fish, and vegetable until the price barometer has plummeted and is set fair so you can buy in quantity, then you will know what to do already. You will be doing it.

You'll have scrumptious pots in your pantry or fridge and a freezer full of the joys of spring, summer, and autumn—even in the winter. Even so, you may not have thought of everything.

As I write this in mid-February, the last of my cooking apple store, somewhat bruised and freckled with brown blotches, is still good enough to bake or puree. And the best way to use up last year's homemade orange marmalade—now a little solid in the jar—is to spoon it over the apples before you bake.

I pick pears to spice and Victoria plums from my trees to freeze; the mulberries and quinces, greengages and walnuts are too young to fruit yet. I risk nature's prickly disdain for man by pulling sloes off their spiky branches in the fall and gathering damsons and blackberries from tree, orchard, and hedgerow.

I make slow, sloe gin—if I can possibly resist dipping into it for a couple of winters, the flavor is all the better—likewise the damson. I drench blackberries in vodka or freeze them au naturel ready for Blackberry and apple brown Betty (page 156) and pies.

I buy kilos of tomatoes from the organic farm down the road to make tomato chile jam, and for the jars of oven-dried and slow-roasted whole tomatoes (page 161), which I store and use in the lean, dark months as the year turns.

Black currants and red currants and raspberries come from my canes, but if they didn't I would go to a "pick-your-own." My pantry mentality of squirreling and preserving the best of a season— to surprise people with when the season's over—is getting more and more, well, squirrely as the years go by. There's nothing quite like the pleasure of looking at a fully jarred and bottled pantry shelf.

As each fruit and vegetable ripens there's a brief plethora, so what I don't eat I freeze, preserve, pickle, chutnefy, turn to jam or jelly, or blend and sieve raw—ready for a hit of intense black currant vitamin C in a winter sorbet or ice cream or fool. Each time I open the arctic door and gaze at the purple packets, frosted with rime, it warms the midwinter soul with the comfort of knowing I've got a reminder of summer on a dark, chill night.

The last of the baked apples

I'm not one for the school-lunch corn syrup and currants version. I like to tweak the apple as the year turns. Winter is dried fruit time, so chopped unsulfured apricots pushed down through the core cavity with some sugar and butter and a topknot of my last year's orange marmalade is a possibility. Or some chopped prunes and broken walnuts with apricot jam splodged on top and perhaps a hint of Armagnac or crumbled almondy amaretti packed inside with the fruit.

Before stuffing, score the apples around their circumference to stop them from bursting during baking, pry out the cores almost to the base, and brush the skins with melted butter. Sometimes I also roll the apples in light muscovado or raw sugar flavored with freshly ground cinnamon and allspice. Stand the apples on a baking tray and fill the cavities generously. Give them 30 minutes in a preheated fairly hot oven, say 350 degrees F, until they feel soft right through when tested with a skewer. Serve this easiest and most comforting of desserts with whipped cream, homemade crème anglaise, or good vanilla ice cream.

Stewed plums

I usually put my frozen plums straight into an earthenware dish, turn them in sugar— preferably muscovado, for its affinity with the fruit— and add half cinnamon stick and 2 tablespoons dark rum. That is it.

I allow ⅔ cup of muscovado or brown sugar to 2 pounds of my Victoria plums, since they are an eating plum, and anyway I don't like things oversweetened. Trust to taste, your own—you can always add a little more after cooking but, as they say, you can't take it away.

Cook the plums from frozen, uncovered, in a preheated oven at 300 degrees F, and start checking after 40 minutes. Adjust the sweetness if you need to.

Blackberry and apple brown Betty

This cooktop Betty involves a mere 10 minutes with butter, sugar, fruit, and crumbs. And perhaps a little liqueur—cassis goes well with this, or a little kirsch. Or, if you make this with plums, rum or whiskey is lovely. You can either cook the apples to a puree, which happens anyway with many cooking apples, or slice and fry eating apples in butter, as I've done here, adding the blackberries toward the end.

Serves 4.

for the crumb topping

3 or 4 slices good stale brown or white bread, crusts removed

4 tablespoons (½ stick) unsalted butter

1 teaspoon freshly ground cinnamon, or more

2 or 3 whole allspice, crushed

1 to 2 heaping tablespoons light muscovado or other sugar

for the fruit

4 good, large, tart apples, such as McIntosh

2 tablespoons (¼ stick) unsalted butter

1 tablespoon unrefined granulated sugar

a couple of handfuls of blackberries (or raspberries in season)

1 to 2 tablespoons crème de cassis or kirsch

For the topping, tear the bread to crumbs. Melt the butter in a large skillet until foaming, then throw in the bread crumbs and stir to coat them all over. Now stir sporadically over gentle to medium heat so the crumbs crisp all over, but do not let them turn dark brown. You cannot hurry this.

Meanwhile, peel, core, and slice the apples. Cook them with the butter and sugar in another pan, stirring every so often, until softened. Before they collapse, throw in the blackberries and cassis, and stir for a few more minutes. (If you use cooking apples, just add more sugar to taste and cook them to a puree before you add the berries.) Once the apples and blackberries are cooked, remove them from the heat.

To finish the topping, add the cinnamon, allspice, and muscovado sugar to the crisp crumbs and stir briefly to melt the sugar. Now taste: to get the spicing right you may need up to another 1 teaspoon cinnamon. Remove from the heat.

Give everybody a generous spoonful or two of fruit and scatter the hot spicy crumb on top. Serve it with some heavy cream—either unwhipped (as shown) or whipped.

Black currant or blackberry sorbet

Raw black currants are one of my favorite fruits. That starburst of raw taste smacks tongue and taste buds into total, salivatory submission in an instant. And the slightly musty note in the scent only adds to the little black bauble's naked charms.

I froze bags of raw black currant puree last summer and, astonishingly, its zing factor and color are barely lessened by seven months shut away in the cold. The thrill of a black currant out-of-season sorbet is every bit as exciting in winter, when one most craves currants, berries, and stone fruit, as it is in the summer when we have them on a plate. If you can't get fresh black currants, this sorbet is equally good made with blackberries.

Serves 8 to 10.

1 pound black currants or blackberries, stripped of their stems

2 cups water

1 cup unrefined superfine vanilla sugar

a spritz of lemon juice

Put the black currants or blackberries in the food processor or blender and blend them to a purple velvet puree. Push through a sieve into a large bowl with a wooden spoon, only discarding the dry, seedy pulp that won't go through. This calls for a little muscle power. (This is the raw puree that I freeze so much of.)

Put the water and sugar in a pan and bring to a boil, then continue to boil for 5 minutes. Cool the sugar syrup in a heatproof bowl set in a larger bowl of ice, or just let it cool slowly.

Introduce three-quarters of the sugar syrup to the puree and taste. Remember that all things churned taste sweeter, so at this stage it should be sharp. Add a spritz of lemon juice to accentuate the flavor of the fruit and taste again. You may need to add more of the sugar syrup, you may need another spritz of lemon juice, it may be perfect. Adjust accordingly.

Churn the mixture in an ice-cream machine until firm. If you do not have one, freeze in a suitable container, whisking every 30 minutes or so to break down the ice crystals.

Either serve the sorbet right away or keep in a sealed container in the freezer, taking it out about 10 minutes before serving to soften slightly. As with all fruit sorbets, the flavor diminishes quite quickly, so eat within the week. Accompany with little butter cookies (page 53), flavoring them with lavender if it is in season.

Oven-dried tomatoes

Drying tomatoes like this intensifies the flavor to the most delectable degree and gives you something special to add to a tomato sauce or use alone. The addition of a few herbs and a little good olive oil gives you the very simplest of pasta sauces. Combine oven-dried with slow-roasted tomatoes and you have double delicious.

Use the best-flavored tomatoes you can find—cherry, plum, or another larger variety. There is no point in my giving you a quantity; it is up to you entirely. Slice the tomatoes in half and spread them out, cut side up, on a baking sheet. Add a tiny sliver of garlic, a scrunch of salt, a turn of pepper, and a few thyme leaves to each and top with a few drops of good olive oil.

I leave mine on the warm plate on top of my Aga range, but you can achieve a similar effect in a conventional oven, using the lowest setting. After a few hours, when the tomatoes are wrinkling, turn them over. Repeat until the tomatoes are dried but not shriveled. Mine usually take 24 hours on the Aga; they may take more or less in a conventional oven.

Decant to a sterilized screw-top or mason jar, pour good olive oil over to cover, and seal. Store somewhere cool and not sunlit. Use within four months and refrigerate once opened. The oil is then beautifully flavored to cook with, or to use again.

Slow-roasted whole tomatoes

Use full-flavored ripe cherry or plum tomatoes or another, larger variety. Pack as many tomatoes as you want to use—tightly but not squeezed together—in a roasting pan or earthenware dish and drizzle over a modest few drops of olive oil.

As for the dried tomato slices, use the lowest setting of the oven. The tomatoes will take 3 to 4 hours. The tomatoes should shrivel up, looking like someone one hundred years old, complexion-wise. Check how they are doing every hour until you have the desired cosmetic effect.

When ready, cool to warm and decant into sterilized jars with sealed tops or screw tops and pour good olive oil over them to cover. Seal and store somewhere cool and not sunlit. Use within four months and refrigerate once opened.

Tomato chile jam

I make no apologies for recycling this recipe from my Kitchen Bible, *particularly since it is somewhat modified. We obsessive cooks tinker and tweak for amusement, so as not to get stuck in a cooking rut and since we are always in search of that elusive thing, the perfect recipe.*

I make batches of this right through the tomato season and give it away, usually over-generously, until I'm left with not enough until the season reappears. I eat it without ever tiring, on Lancashire, Cheddar, and single Gloucester cheese, with goat cheese and Caerphilly, and spooned onto roasted squashes, red onion, and sweet potato. I have even been known to deck the occasional scallop with it.

Makes 3 x 1-pound jars.

4 pounds very ripe tomatoes

4 medium red chiles, with their seeds

2 Scotch bonnet (very hot) chiles, with their seeds

2 green chiles, with their seeds

10 fat garlic cloves, peeled

piece of fresh ginger approx. 5 x ¼", peeled and roughly chopped

⅓ cup Thai fish sauce

3 cups (scant) unrefined superfine sugar

1 cup (scant) red wine vinegar

Chop half of the tomatoes into small dice and set aside. Put the rest of the tomatoes with the chiles and their seeds, garlic, ginger, and fish sauce in a blender and blend to a fine puree.

Spoon the puree into a deep, heavy-bottomed pan and add the sugar and wine vinegar. Bring to a boil slowly, stirring as you go. When it comes to a boil, turn down to a simmer and add the diced tomatoes. Skim off any foam that rises to the surface and cook gently for up to 1½ hours, stirring from time to time, to prevent the mixture from sticking and burning. Scrape the sides of the pot too, so that everything cooks evenly. The mixture thickens as it cooks—as it reduces and as the pectin in the tomatoes takes effect.

When the mixture seems thick to the stir of a wooden spoon, decant it through a large funnel into hot, sterilized jars and seal.

Store in a larder or cool place, not the fridge, for up to 9 months, though you are unlikely to make it last beyond Christmas. Once opened, keep in the fridge.

Something-out-

I have no idea what's for supper tonight. That's normal for me, I'm not the sort of person who color codes her clothes drawers and works out her menu a month in advance. I like a challenge, a spur, particularly after shopping and cooking for the weekend. As I open the fridge door when I stop work tonight, I know there'll be something to turn into a great supper. Something out of nothing.

It's Monday morning and there are three days left to cook on-the-trot before Thursday's farmers' market, a trip to my fish shop late morning when the boats come in, to the deli, and to the supermarket. This chapter is about working with what you've got and thinking about shopping and storing so you've always got it.

Consider this. If you can't cook a week's worth of dinners out of what you have in your pantry, in fridge, freezer, and garden or window box, then something, somewhere, is wrong. Letting your stores run down or shopping daily is a false economy, both time- and money-wise, and leads to despair and panic buying, to expensive mistakes, to ready-mades and quick-cooks and a generally less imaginative way of cooking and eating.

Be prepared. For feast rather than famine, that is. It feels so much better to know that the fridge is stocked with standbys,

of-nothing suppers

from tahini and preserved lemons to mustards and a whole range
of different cheeses; with a panoply of half-full condiments or
their unopened brethren in the pantry.

Then there are the legumes and pastas, polentas and rices, oils
and vinegars; I won't go on. Common sense in the kitchen is not
so common these days—the persuasive powers of the supermarket
would lead us into temptation down every aisle. But be bold and
resolute, stick to the stove, learn to love your leftovers, and cook
when there's nothing in the house.

If the horrifying statistic that we throw away 30 percent of the
food we buy is true, we can live better for less if we only incorporate yesterday's leftovers into tonight's supper. When I offer a
lemon risotto to my children, or homemade baked beans, or a tart
made with leek tops and the ends of an old goat cheese, they are
as content as they would be with a chop and some veggies.

I always try to have a lump of fresh yeast for a pizza or bread;
it really isn't any trouble to make either. And the pantry is a
treasure-house to plunder for a pizza—made with a little leftover
tomato sauce, my favorite charcoal-grilled artichokes, roasted
peppers (also from a jar), good olives or olive paste, capers,
mozzarella, and salami.

A chickpea curry that my daughter Charissa learned last year,
while working in an orphanage in the Himalayas, has entered
the repertoire as a staple. Once the roles have been reversed and
your children start cooking for you, you have another pleasure in
store—not just their food and a night off, but a chance to encourage and teach them how to make something out of nothing so that
they, too, are equipped not just for student life, but for life itself.

Chickpea masala

When my younger daughter Charissa went to work in an orphanage in the foothills of the Himalayas last year, all the food was grown on the nearby family farm. She learned to cook with Mrs. Khani, who ran the place with her husband and prepared everything every day from scratch, from the chapattis to the wonderful vegetarian dishes indigenous to the region. Charissa came back with all the recipes in a little booklet. Here are the ones we love best.

Serve them all together with spiced basmati rice and your favorite curry accompaniments. Raita, sliced banana sprinkled with fried onion seeds and crushed cardamom, and a good mango chutney won't go amiss.

Serves 4.

2 cups dried chickpeas, previously soaked in cold water for at least 8 hours

2 tablespoons olive oil

1 onion, peeled and sliced

¼ teaspoon ground turmeric

1 teaspoon chile powder

½ teaspoon ground coriander

1 teaspoon coarse salt

1 tablespoon ginger and garlic paste (fresh ginger and garlic pounded together)

4 large tomatoes, chopped

½ teaspoon garam masala

a handful of cilantro leaves, chopped

Drain the soaked chickpeas and place them in a pan. Add enough water to cover by about ¾", but don't add salt at this stage. Bring to a boil, cover, and lower the heat. Simmer for 1½ to 2 hours until tender.

Heat the olive oil in a skillet over medium heat, then add the onion and cook until golden and softened.

Meanwhile, in a blender or food processor, blend the turmeric, chile powder, ground coriander, salt, ginger and garlic paste, and one of the chopped tomatoes with a little water to form a paste.

Add this masala paste to the onion and cook over medium heat for 5 to 10 minutes until the color darkens and the oil comes to the surface. Stir in the chickpeas, then cover and simmer gently for 15 minutes.

Add the rest of the tomatoes, garam masala, and chopped cilantro and heat for a few minutes.

Aloo palak (Spiced potato and spinach)

Serves 4.

2 tablespoons olive oil

2 garlic cloves, peeled and sliced

2 green chiles, sliced

1 teaspoon ground turmeric

coarse salt

1 pound spinach, washed and chopped

2 medium potatoes, peeled and cubed

2 tomatoes, chopped

Heat the olive oil in a wok or skillet over medium heat. When hot, add the sliced garlic and cook until it just begins to color, then add the chiles with their seeds. Cook for about 5 minutes until the chiles start to darken, then sprinkle with the turmeric and salt and cook for a few seconds.

Add the chopped spinach and cubed potatoes, mix well, and cook for 2 minutes. Stir in the chopped tomatoes, then cover and cook for 20 minutes or until the potatoes are tender.

Mint chutney

If you do not have any tamarind paste in your pantry, you can make a simple fresh chutney by blending the mint leaves with a little lemon juice and adjusting to taste.

Serves 4.

4 handfuls mint leaves
4 handfuls cilantro leaves
3 garlic cloves, peeled
3 green chiles
1 teaspoon coarse salt
2 tablespoons tamarind juice
½ teaspoon toasted cumin seeds

Process everything together in a blender, then taste and adjust the seasoning if you need to. Scrape into a serving bowl.

For the tamarind juice, you will need to soak
1 tablespoon tamarind paste in 2 tablespoons boiling
water for about 10 minutes, then strain to remove
the seeds. Toast the cumin seeds briefly in a hot, dry
pan until they just change color, about 30 seconds.

Japanese squash gnocchi
with sage butter

Whenever I make gnocchi I wonder why I don't make them more often. They are deceptively easy to get right and make you feel proud each time they rise magically in the simmering water. And they turn out as light as a cloud, yet as substantial as you could wish for.

These little pillows of cheesy, nutmeggy squash are dressed with salty, sharp pecorino and Parmesan and coated in glossy butter with lovely aromatic fried sage leaves. A radicchio salad with some watercress and a little Boston lettuce, dressed with best balsamic vinegar and olive oil, is the only accompaniment you'll need.

Serves 2.

1 Japanese (Uchiki Kuri) squash, about ½ pound

a little olive oil

¾ to 1 cup "00" Italian flour

1 teaspoon baking powder

coarse salt and black pepper

1 organic large egg

4 tablespoons freshly grated aged Parmigiano-Reggiano

nutmeg for grating

12 young, soft sage leaves

2 to 3 tablespoons unsalted butter, plus an extra knob to serve if you like

2 tablespoons freshly grated pecorino, or extra Parmesan if that's all you have

Preheat the oven to 400 degrees F. Halve the squash and scoop out the seeds with a spoon, then place both halves, cut side down, on a lightly oiled baking sheet. Roast for 45 minutes or until tender when pierced through with a skewer. Lower the oven setting to 325 degrees F.

Scoop out the cooked pulp and push it through the coarse disk of a food mill, or through a potato ricer, into a large bowl. If it seems wet, dry it out by stirring it in a pan over medium heat for a few minutes, then place in the bowl.

Sift in ¾ cup of the flour with the baking powder and 1 teaspoon salt and break the egg into the mixture. Mix well and add 2 tablespoons Parmesan and a grating of nutmeg—slightly more than the usual restrained grating. The mixture will be tacky and sticky, so it will stick to your hands, but add more flour only if it seems runny.

Bring a large, heavy-bottomed pan of salted water to a boil. Meanwhile, with floured hands, shape the dough into small tablespoonfuls. Dunk them in a little more flour to coat all over, shaking off the excess, and plop them onto a large plate.

Roll up the sage leaves together and slice thinly to cut them into long, thin shreds. Melt the butter in a pan, add the sage, and heat until it turns crisp, not letting the butter brown.

Warm a large, greased au gratin dish in the oven. Drop half of the gnocchi into the boiling water with a spoon, spacing them apart, and keep the water at a gentle simmer. The gnocchi will take longer than you think to start rising to the surface but they will, and when they do, allow them another 3 minutes, then scoop them out with a slotted spoon and plop them into the au gratin dish with a little of their cooking water to keep them moist. You can pour the sage butter on top and sprinkle with a little of the remaining Parmesan and pecorino at this stage, too. Pop them into the oven to keep warm.

Cook the second batch of gnocchi and then add them to the au gratin dish. Sprinkle with more cheese and serve on warmed plates with the rest of the cheese in a bowl alongside. Scrunch pepper over the gnocchi and top with a little knob of butter, if you feel like it, before you bring the dish to the table.

Spanish tortilla

The classic Spanish tortilla is a simple egg, potato, and olive oil affair, but I usually add to it a red and green layer of roasted bell peppers and wilted spinach, and often a tangle of softened onions, too. Unlike a normal omelet, a tortilla will keep for a couple of days. You can eat it hot, warm, or cold, or reheat it in some Romesco or tomato sauce. One of the best dishes to take on a picnic.

Serves 4.

1 pound potatoes, peeled
coarse salt and black pepper
3 to 4 tablespoons good fruity olive oil
6 organic large eggs

flavorings (optional)

2 large onions, peeled and thinly sliced

a little olive oil

2 red bell peppers, charred or roasted and skinned, cored, and seeded, or a handful of piquillo peppers from a jar

1 pound spinach, washed

to serve (optional)

Romesco (page 113), pureed rather than coarse-textured, or any homemade tomato sauce (page 174)

Add the potatoes to a pot of salted water and parboil for 10 minutes or so until almost *al dente*. Drain and cut into small cubes when cool enough to handle. Choose a skillet that is deep rather than wide, and oil the bottom and sides. Add 2 to 3 tablespoons olive oil and place over moderate heat. When hot, add the cubed potatoes and cook gently on all sides until tender, but don't allow them to color.

In the meantime, prepare the flavorings, if using. Cook the onions in a little olive oil until very soft. Cut the peppers into strips. Cook the spinach in a pan with just the water clinging to the leaves after washing until it just collapses, then place in a sieve and press with the back of a spoon to remove the water.

Beat the eggs in a bowl and season them. Cover the potatoes with the onion slices and strips of red pepper, then strew the spinach over the surface, if using. Pour in the beaten eggs and cook over high heat for a minute, then turn the heat down and let the tortilla cook slowly, right through. Shake the pan a little to make sure it doesn't stick.

When you see that the top of the egg is no longer liquid, even in the middle, cover the pan with a large, flat plate and invert the tortilla onto it. Add another 1 tablespoon olive oil to the pan, slide the tortilla back in, and cook for another minute or two.

Slide the finished tortilla out onto a large, warmed plate. Serve as it is, or with some well-pureed Romesco or tomato sauce.

If flipping the tortilla is too daunting, once the top is set put the pan under the broiler for a few minutes and let the tortilla brown and puff up a little.

Paella with spring vegetables

They may be called spring vegetables, but in these cold climes, where I live, they are generally available in the early summer. Asparagus is the first to arrive, with its short six-week season, in late spring.

You can change the ingredients as they come and go, from artichokes to snow peas, baby zucchini to young carrots and turnips, remembering that all paellas traditionally incorporate some part of a pig. So unless you don't eat pig, a little pancetta or bacon works beautifully here with the shellfish and spring vegetables. Or if you have some chorizo sitting in the fridge, use it instead and you'll find it colors the dish a lovely brick red.

I like to use the traditional Spanish Calasparra rice for a paella, but Italian risotto rice is an option if that's what you have in your pantry. As for timing, the rice takes around 25 minutes to cook.

Serves 6.

1 pound mussels or Manila shell clams, or a mixture of both, plus 1 pound monkfish fillet, cubed

4 tablespoons olive oil

1 large onion, peeled and chopped

6 ounces unsmoked bacon or pancetta, cut into small strips

2 garlic cloves, peeled and minced

6 baby carrots

3½ cups chicken stock

²/₃ cup dry white wine

2¼ cups Calasparra rice

a small bunch of flat-leaf parsley, leaves chopped

large pinch of saffron threads

6 asparagus spears, woody ends snapped off, cut into short lengths

¾ cup shelled baby fava beans (blanched and skinned if any larger)

¾ cup (scant) shelled fresh peas

6 baby zucchini, cut in half

2 large tomatoes, skinned, seeded, and chopped

coarse salt and black pepper

Scrub the mussels and clams thoroughly in cold water, removing the beards from the mussels and discarding any mussels or clams with open shells that do not close when sharply tapped. Set aside in a bowl of cold, salted water.

Heat the olive oil in a paella pan or large, heavy-bottomed skillet, then add the onion and bacon and fry over moderate heat until the onion begins to soften. Add the garlic and carrots and turn to coat in the oil for a few minutes. Meanwhile, bring the stock and wine to a boil in another pan and lower the heat to a simmer; keep it like this throughout the cooking process.

Add the rice and half the parsley to the paella pan and stir to coat in the oil. Then add about a quarter of the stock and wine, throw in your saffron, and stir it in. As soon as the liquid has been absorbed by the rice, pour in another quarter, adding the asparagus at this stage. When this has been absorbed, add the third quarter, along with the fava beans and peas.

Add the zucchini with the last of the stock and wine, and throw in the chopped tomatoes and shellfish, along with the monkfish. Cover the pan now, just until the shellfish have opened, which will take only a few minutes. Season, then taste and adjust. Once the rice is cooked, take the pan off the heat and leave the paella, covered, for 5 minutes to allow the flavors to marry.

Remove the lid, sprinkle the rest of the chopped parsley over, and serve straight from the pan.

Broiled sardines or mackerel
with green and black olive salsa

Fresh sardines, like fresh mackerel, are hard to come by in England. Both are the sort of oily fish that need to be eaten on the day they were pulled from the deep. I do this with mackerel in the summer in the west of Ireland because I pull them out of the deep myself, or my neighbors come around with some of them they've gone out and caught. However, with sardines, I tend to opt for frozen ones if I see them—Portuguese sardines are frozen the moment they hit the deck and are nearly as good as the fresh. I buy them by the bag for pasta con le sarde—a lovely baked pasta, fennel, and sardine dish flavored with anchovies, raisins, and pine nuts—and for this lovely Provençal-inspired dish.

Serves 4.

5 or 6 sardines (or 1 mackerel) per person
olive oil for brushing
coarse salt and black pepper

for the olive salsa
about 4 tablespoons good, peppery olive oil
6 large green olives, pitted and sliced
8 to 10 smaller Taggiasca or Nyons olives, halved and pitted
24 cherry tomatoes, halved
a handful of basil leaves, chopped
grated zest and juice of 1 organic lemon

to serve
tomato balsamico (page 174), warm

Make the olive salsa about 30 minutes ahead so that the flavors get a chance to mingle. Pour the olive oil into a bowl and throw in the olives, together with the tomatoes, chopped basil, and lemon zest and juice. Toss all together and repeat just before you use it.

Meanwhile, using a knife, scrape the scales from the sardines over the sink. You must do this thoroughly, then rinse the fish under cold water and feel for any stray scales with your fingers. Behead and gut the fish, unless your fish seller has done it for you, by cutting a small slit from just below the head on the underside of each fish to the belly, where it swells, and removing the innards. Wash again under cold water. Press the central backbone right down its length and remove it. (If you are using mackerel, fillet the fish, cutting on either side of the spine to release the two fillets.) Check the fish thoroughly for any small bones.

Place the sardines in a baking dish, skin side up, and brush them all with a little olive oil. Season and place under a hot broiler for about 5 minutes until bubbling and the skin has started to blacken and blister in patches. (If you are cooking mackerel, just keep them under the broiler for about another 5 minutes, skin side up throughout.) The magical, oily juices that collect in the bottom of the dish are to be poured back over the fish, not thrown away.

Place a good spoonful of warm tomato balsamico on each warmed plate and lay the broiled sardines (or mackerel) on top. Spoon some of the olive salsa onto the side of each plate and serve the rest separately in a bowl. Alternatively, present all the fish together on a large platter.

Tomato balsamico

Tomato sauce is possibly the most versatile sauce in the world. It works with chunks of white fish, with meatballs and meat loaf, with stuffed vegetables, and with pasta and a host of other pantry items for easy suppers (see right). This is really just a jazzed-up version of an everyday tomato sauce, easily assembled from ingredients you are likely to have on hand.

Serves 4.

3 tablespoons olive oil

1 onion, peeled and minced

3 garlic cloves, peeled and minced

14-ounce can diced tomatoes

1 tablespoon tomato paste

2 tablespoons good aged balsamic vinegar

a long strip of orange zest from an organic orange

coarse salt and black pepper

Heat the olive oil in a pan over medium heat until hot, then throw in the onion and garlic and cook until softened and pale golden, about 10 minutes.

Add the canned tomatoes, tomato paste, balsamic vinegar, orange zest, and some seasoning. Bring to a simmer and bubble at a burble, nothing too fast and furious, until the liquid has mostly evaporated from around the tomatoes but they are still whole, about 10 to 15 minutes. Taste and adjust the seasoning if you need to.

Tomato sauce with carrot, basil, and cream

Any riff on a tomato sauce is worth adding to your repertoire. And this one gives you the option of using fresh or canned plum tomatoes. It freezes well with either, though I normally never get it as far as the freezer. I cook it one night and leave it in the fridge to use in something else the next day or later in the week.

Serves 6.

3¼ pounds fresh ripe tomatoes in season, or 3 x 14-ounce cans whole plum tomatoes

6 tablespoons (¾ stick) unsalted butter

6 tablespoons very finely diced carrots

1 medium onion, peeled and finely minced

2 celery stalks, strings removed with a potato peeler and finely minced

coarse salt and black pepper

1 tablespoon olive oil (if using canned tomatoes)

⅔ cup heavy cream

a handful of basil leaves

If using fresh tomatoes, cut in half vertically and put them in a heavy-bottomed pan over medium heat. As they begin to cook, put the lid on and turn the heat down a little. Cook gently for 10 minutes, then push the tomatoes through the coarse disk of a food mill. Return to the pan and add the rest of the ingredients, except the cream and half the basil. Cook, uncovered, at a mere shudder for 45 to 60 minutes, giving the pan an occasional stir to stop anything from sticking.

If you are using canned tomatoes, start the carrots, onion, and celery off in a little olive oil to soften them a bit. Meanwhile, put the canned tomatoes straight through the food mill and then add them to the pan. Cook as above.

Add the cream, turn the heat up a little, and stir at a bubble for a minute or two. Remove from the heat, check the seasoning, and tear in the rest of the basil leaves.

Tomato sauce with pantry additions

The tomato balsamico and tomato, carrot, and basil cream sauce, opposite, both lend themselves to a variety of pantry suppers if you have the right ingredients on hand.

Sometimes you want a sauce as coarse as nature intended it for a simple pasta dish or to douse some homemade mozzarella meatballs. At other times you want a slightly smoother texture, best achieved by putting the sauce through the coarse disk of a food mill. This is the texture I prefer for a pizza topping.

Sometimes you will want to pep up your tomato sauce with a few chile flakes or shakes of Tabasco to make an arrabiatta pasta sauce. Or you will add black olives, chiles, anchovies, capers, and perhaps a little black olive paste, for a puttanesca. Crumbled tuna also works well in a basic tomato sauce; the ventresca (belly) is best.

For the pasta dish below, I used some leftover filling from the autumn lasagna (page 70),

tossing in a few spoonfuls of leftover tomato sauce along with some oven-dried tomatoes and a handful of slow-roasted tomatoes (page 161) from the pantry.

If your pantry contains a bag of lovely golden polenta, try using this instead of pasta for a puttanesca, stirring in some Parmesan and butter. You can drape a branch or two of roasted vine tomatoes on top of the sauce on each plate, too, to spruce it up. Or add roasted sliced eggplant to the tomato sauce; simply brush the eggplant with olive oil and roast on a baking sheet in the oven at 400 degrees F for 15 minutes first.

There really is no end to the charm of a tomato sauce, and it is worth always keeping your options open by having all the aforementioned ingredients in your pantry—like a kind of culinary first-aid kit—for all eventualities, for a something-out-of-nothing night.

Salade Niçoise

The great thing about this vibrant, Technicolored dream of a many-layered dish is that you just put in whatever you have in the summer season, whatever is at its best. And you can choose to include cooked, charcoal-grilled, or raw ingredients, depending on your pantry and your time. Any leftovers can go into my favorite summer sandwich the next day, the mighty pan bagna (page 179).

Serves 6.

4 tomatoes

½ pound green beans, ends trimmed

coarse salt and black pepper

1 small cucumber

1 red bell pepper

1 yellow bell pepper

1 large garlic clove, peeled and crushed

juice of 1½ or 2 lemons

6 tablespoons good olive oil

1 Boston lettuce, washed

a small handful of basil leaves

a few sprigs of parsley

6 grilled artichoke hearts, or cooked baby artichokes

7 to 9 scallions, trimmed and sliced

6 large radishes, halved, a little green top left on

6 organic large eggs

6-ounce can good-quality tuna (ideally ventresca), in olive oil

a large handful of olives, preferably Nyons, pitted

12 good-quality anchovy fillets, rinsed and drained

Core the tomatoes and cut them into quarters, or chop them smaller if they are very big.

Throw the green beans into a pot of boiling, salted water and cook until just softer than *al dente*, then immediately drain and refresh under cold water to retain their color and crunch. Peel the cucumber, halve lengthwise, and scoop out the seeds, then cut into sticks.

Hold the peppers over a flame with a pair of tongs or broil them until scorched and charred all over, then put into a bowl and cover with plastic wrap to encourage the steam to lift the skins. When cool enough to handle, peel the peppers and remove the core and seeds, then slice them into strips.

For the dressing, put the garlic in the salad serving bowl and pour the lemon juice and olive oil into the bowl. Season with salt and pepper. Whisk using a small whisk or fork, and taste and adjust the seasoning.

Tear the lettuce, basil, and parsley leaves into the salad bowl. Add the tomatoes, beans, cucumber, peppers, cooked baby artichokes, if using, scallions, and radishes, and toss together very gently. Leave to stand for 30 minutes to an hour.

In the meantime, boil the eggs for 6 to 7 minutes, depending on size, so they are the soft side of hard-boiled. Drain and cool under cold water, then peel and halve.

Toss the salad in the bowl, again gently, then crumble in the tuna and add the olives and artichokes (if using chargrilled from a jar). Add the halved eggs, anchovies, and a little more olive oil. Scrunch over a little pepper and a sprinkling of salt, but go easy, as anchovies are salty.

Pan bagna

You may engineer leftovers of the salade Niçoise on the previous page by making it for fewer people, or by upping the quantities.

Split a fresh baguette or ciabatta in half horizontally and, using your fingers, scoop out some of the crumb, not all, from the lower side of the loaf. Rub the cut sides with garlic and sprinkle a tiny bit of red wine vinegar or tarragon vinegar on top.

Pile the Niçoise filling into the excavated side and sprinkle with more olive oil, seasoning, and chopped basil. Oil the cut surface of the top half before closing it down onto the pile of goodies. Wrap in foil and weight down overnight in the fridge.

The following day, allow the pan bagna to come back to room temperature out of the foil before eating. Perfect picnic food.

Leek and potato patty
with blood sausage and cheese

A paupery of ingredients in the vegetable rack and fridge, but a wonder of a simple, comforting supper is lurking there. Half a blood sausage left over from the stuffed pork fillet with figs and Marsala (page 143) inspired this recipe. Bubbling with good cheese and richly flavored with leeks and blood sausage, this potato cake needs nothing else, unless you feel like a romaine salad on the side.

Serves 2.

1 pound potatoes, peeled
coarse salt and black pepper
1 tablespoon olive oil
2 tablespoons butter
2 leeks, washed and both green and white chopped
½ blood sausage, approx. ¼ pound
a little milk
about 1 ounce blue-veined cheese
about 1 ounce grated Comté, Gruyère, or similar cheese
1 tablespoon freshly grated Parmesan

Preheat the oven to 375 degrees F. Boil the potatoes in salted water in the usual way. In the meantime, heat the olive oil and 1 tablespoon butter in a pan and sauté the chopped leeks until softened. Crumble in the blood sausage and fry, stirring, for a few minutes.

When the potatoes are cooked, drain and mash them with the remaining butter and a little milk. Place half of the potatoes in a small-medium, heavy-bottomed skillet with an ovenproof handle and flatten. Pile the leek and blood sausage mixture on top.

Crumble the blue cheese over the surface and top with the grated Comté. Cover with the rest of the potatoes, flatten, and sprinkle with the Parmesan and a scrunch of pepper. Bake for 25 minutes until bubbling, oozing, and golden.

Supper, for a song, in a pan.

Boston-baked cranberry beans

Deep flavors, deep and dark; sticky, intense, and as savory and piquant and mellow as you could wish for, this is the best version of the dish I have come up with. My take has blackstrap molasses and molasses sugar, clear honey, tamari, tomato, and mustard, along with star anise. Classically, this dish is made with ham hocks, so you might like to add some pancetta or lardons, fried until the fat begins to run, or just keep it veggie. Cranberry beans retain their shape and texture well, so they are ideal for this dish.

Start the day before, as you need to soak the beans first, or soak them in the morning and get cracking in the early afternoon.

Perfect with sausages and mashed potatoes, or just mashed potatoes.

Serves 4.

1¼ cups cranberry beans or black-eyed peas, previously soaked in cold water for at least 8 hours

a sprig of rosemary

2 bay leaves

1 onion, peeled and stuck with 2 cloves

14-ounce can diced tomatoes

1 heaping tablespoon blackstrap molasses

1 tablespoon honey

1 level tablespoon muscovado or dark brown sugar

1 level tablespoon whole-grain mustard

1 tablespoon tamari sauce

a few shakes of Tabasco

1 star anise

5 white peppercorns

8 to 10 thin slivers of lardo (optional)

Drain the beans and put them into a medium-small, cast-iron cooking pot or similar pan and add the rosemary, bay leaves, and onion stuck with cloves. Just cover with cold water and bring to a boil, then reduce to a simmer and put the lid on. Either put into a low oven at 300 degrees F or continue to simmer gently on top of the stove for an hour.

Drain the beans and return them to the cooking pot, keeping their water to use for a soup; discard the herbs. Add the tomatoes to the beans. Thin the molasses with 2 tablespoons of the saved hot cooking water and add to the beans with the honey and muscovado sugar. Stir these together a little and then add the mustard, tamari, Tabasco, star anise, and white peppercorns.

Bring just to a boil again, then cover and continue to cook in the oven or slowly on the burner for another hour.

Now remove the lid and turn the oven up to 425 degrees F. The liquid will still be thin at this point. If using lardo, lay the slivers on top of the beans. Continue to cook for up to 3 hours, without a lid, until the liquid has turned into a thick, black, sticky, gooey sauce. You may give the dish a gentle stir once or twice to amalgamate everything as it thickens and darkens. The depth of flavor is sensational.

Baked beans with a green herb and Parmesan crust

Instead of cranberry beans, soak the same quantity of navy beans and cook as above until tender, about an hour. Drain, keeping back a few tablespoons of cooking liquid, then turn them in 3 ladlefuls of homemade tomato sauce (page 174), which may be coarse textured or roughly pureed.

Either use ¼ cup Provençal bread crumbs (page 114) or process the chopped leaves from a large bunch of flat-leaf parsley with some plain dried crumbs to make the crust green. Sprinkle 2 tablespoons Parmesan into the crumb mixture, then scatter it on top of the beans. Dot with butter and bake at 425 degrees F for about 20 to 25 minutes. Eat with or without sausages and a baked potato, if you like.

Baked penne with eggplant and tomatoes

A simple, lustrous peasant dish from Puglia, which has the satisfaction principle at heart.
I don't see any need to salt the eggplants before roasting.

Serves 6.

2 large eggplants, cut into small dice

olive oil to drizzle

coarse salt and black pepper

1 pound penne or similar pasta

small knob of butter, the size of a walnut

3 ladlefuls (about 1½ cups) any homemade tomato sauce (page 174)

1½ pounds good tomatoes, sliced

1½ cups bread crumbs

¾ cup grated Parmesan or pecorino, or a mixture

a few sprigs of basil, leaves torn

Preheat the oven to 350 degrees F. Throw the eggplant cubes into a bowl and drizzle over enough olive oil to coat them. Season and toss well, then scatter the cubes on a baking sheet and bake for 15 minutes or until they feel tender when tested with a skewer.

In the meantime, bring a large pot of salted water to a boil. Add the pasta and cook to the slightly firmer side of *al dente*. Drain, holding back a few tablespoons of the cooking water. Return it to the pan with the reserved water and add the knob of butter. Fold in half of the tomato sauce at this point.

Lay half of the tomato slices over the base of an oiled au gratin dish. Sprinkle half the bread crumbs over the top and season. Layer half the tomatoey pasta on top, followed by half the cubed eggplant.

Spread a quarter of the remaining tomato sauce on top, then sprinkle half the grated cheese and half the torn basil over. Now add the remaining pasta, then the rest of the eggplant and tomato sauce.

Scatter the rest of the cheese and the basil over and add the final layer of tomatoes. Sprinkle with the remaining bread crumbs and drizzle over some extra olive oil. Bake for 45 minutes to 1 hour. The dish should be deliciously crusted, bubbling, and brown on top.

Leave to stand for 10 to 15 minutes before serving. The flavors develop and intensify as the dish begins to cool.

Pasta con la Mollica

Simple pasta with bread crumbs, tomatoes, parsley, and anchovies, this is definitely a pantry supper. It is important to use crunchy bread crumbs, made from stale, good crustless bread, toasted in a warm oven on a baking tray until crisp.

Serves 4.

4 to 6 tablespoons olive oil

2 garlic cloves, peeled and thinly sliced

1 celery stalk, strings removed with a potato peeler and finely chopped

1 dried Kashmiri chile, crumbled, or 1 teaspoon dried chile flakes

2 tablespoons chopped flat-leaf parsley

14-ounce can diced tomatoes

1 pound spaghetti or linguine

coarse salt and black pepper

8 anchovies, chopped

1 teaspoon dried oregano

2 tablespoons pitted and sliced green olives

4 heaping tablespoons good dried bread crumbs

knob of butter (optional)

Heat 2 tablespoons olive oil in a large heavy-bottomed skillet and add the garlic, celery, crumbled chile, and parsley. Sauté over medium heat for a couple of minutes, then throw in the tomatoes and cook more briskly, stirring, for 10 minutes.

Meanwhile, add the pasta to a pot of boiling, salted water and cook until *al dente.*

Add the chopped anchovies, oregano, and olives to the tomato mixture and cook for another few minutes. Drain the pasta when it is ready and slip it into the skillet, stirring to mix everything together.

Add the toasted bread crumbs and continue to cook for another minute. Taste for seasoning. Add more oil if the dish needs it and, if you like, a knob of butter. I always add butter, even to an olive oil-based pasta sauce.

Pizza

Pizza is not just a dish, it is an activity, a family thing, a start of the weekend, Friday-night thing, which is so much easier than it seems and so much more satisfying than commercially made pizza. Everyone joins in, even if only to choose the bits and pieces to anoint the great, flat slipper with, and if you want to fold it over calzone-style, the Italian answer to a pasty, well, just go for it. This is fun cooking, with the sort of ingredients I've always got on hand.

Makes two large pizzas.

for the pizza dough

3½ cups white bread flour

2 teaspoons quick-rise dry yeast

2 teaspoons coarse salt

1 tablespoon olive oil

semolina flour, for dusting

for the toppings

homemade tomato sauce of any kind (page 174), preferably coarse-textured rather than smooth

plus any of the following:

a 14-ounce mozzarella di bufala, torn into chunks

1 or 2 garlic cloves, peeled and cut into slivers

cooked cremini mushrooms

grilled or broiled red bell peppers, skinned and sliced into strips

chargrilled artichoke hearts, from a jar

cubed eggplant, roasted in olive oil

salami or prosciutto slices

green and black olives

tiny capers, rinsed and drained

good-quality anchovies

fresh, coarsely grated Parmesan

olive oil, preferably herb-flavored, for brushing

a few basil leaves, shredded or torn

a glug of extra-virgin olive oil

To make the dough, place the flour straight on your work surface, as all self-respecting Italians do, and add the yeast and salt. Make a well in the middle and pour in the olive oil, followed by 1 cup warm water. Begin to knead by tipping the inside wall of flour into the middle and gathering flour as you go. When it gets difficult to knead, gradually add another ½ cup warm water. Continue until you have a dough.

Turn the dough onto a lightly floured surface and knead for about 10 minutes, stretching it away from you with the heel of your hand every so often, then furling it back toward you with your fingers. Divide in two, shape into balls, and place on an oiled baking sheet. Cover with a plastic bag and leave to rise in a warm place until the balls have doubled in size, about 1½ hours.

Preheat the oven to its highest setting, at least 450 degrees F. Scatter semolina flour over 2 baking sheets. Working with one ball at a time, punch down the dough, stretch it, and then roll it out until about ¼" thick. Don't worry—it will shrink and spring back to begin with, but eventually it will obey your command. Keep the rim a little thicker. Repeat with the other ball of dough.

Spread your tomato sauce generously over the dough, up to the rim, with a spatula. Now add your choice of toppings—any combination you like. If you divide the pizza into four "windows" and fill each one with a different topping, you have a work of art!

Bake the pizzas for 15 minutes before checking. The edges should be brown. Remove from the oven and brush the rim instantly with a little herb-flavored olive oil. A scattering of basil and a drizzle of olive oil on top of the pizza, and it is ready.

> Leftover ratatouille is a good alternative to the tomato sauce topping. Just add olive oil, garlic slivers, thyme or oregano, coarse salt and pepper, and a few dried chile flakes. If you have oven-dried or slow-roasted tomatoes (page 161) on hand, throw some in, too.
>
> For a simple topping, when good tomatoes are around in the summer, blanch and skin 1 pound or so, then chop, discarding the seeds and juice. Cover the pizza dough with the chopped tomatoes, then add oregano, garlic, and olive oil. Simple and sumptuous.

Index

A

almonds
  almond cake with apricot jam 41
  bay, honey, and lemon cake 50
  braised chicken and rice with
    orange, saffron, almonds, and
    pistachio syrup 140
  dried cranberry and cinnamon
    friands 49
  nut brittle 82
  Romesco sauce 112–13
  Spanish chicken with a saffron
    and almond sauce 110
aloo palak (spiced potato and
  spinach) 166
amaretti cookies
  baked peach brown Betty 118
anchovies
  Italian meat loaf 20–21
  little fish fillets with braised fennel
    and anchovy butter 139
  pasta con la Mollica 183
apples
  baked 154
  blackberry and apple brown Betty
    156
  carrot, apple, and blue cheese
    soup 131
  Eva's potato apple cake 24
  pork and apple stuffing 13
apricots
  almond cake with apricot jam 41
  dried apricot upside-down cake
    40
artichokes
  salade Niçoise 176
autumn vegetable lasagna 70

B

bacon
  Italian meat loaf 20–21
  tartiflette 89
baked apples 154
baked beans with a green herb and
  Parmesan crust 180

baked peach brown Betty 118
baking 34–53
balsamic vinegar
  tomato balsamico 174
banana blondies 46
basil, tomato sauce with carrot,
  cream, and 174
bay leaves
  bay, honey, and lemon cake 50
  winter fruit salad 146
beans
  baked beans with a green herb
    and Parmesan crust 180
  Boston-baked cranberry beans 180
beef 54
  beef stew with mustard and
    thyme dumplings 57
  brisket with pickled walnuts and
    celery root 58
  cottage pie 19
  Italian meat loaf 20–21
  oxtail stewed with grapes 59
beets
  roasted and raw beet soup with
    rye 106–107
Belgian endive
  pheasant braised with endive,
    white wine, and crème fraîche
    68
  winter panzanella 98–9
bitter chocolate custards 79
bitter chocolate sorbet 84
blackberry and apple brown Betty
  156
blackberry sorbet 159
black currant sorbet 159
blondies, banana 46
blood sausage
  leek and potato patty with blood
    sausage and cheese 179
  stuffed pork fillet with figs and
    Marsala 143
blue cheese
  carrot, apple, and blue cheese
    soup 131

  spicy chicken wings with blue
    cheese dressing 10
Boston-baked cranberry beans 180
Brazil nuts
  banana blondies 46
bread 92–121
  bread crumbs to coat fish 114
  fried mozzarella sandwich 100
  gazpacho 109
  making bread 94–95
  mushroom soup with spices and
    bread 105
  pa amb oli, pa amb tomàquet 96
  pain perdu with fruit compote
    119
  pan bagna 179
  pancotto (bread soup) 104
  potato bread 23
  Provençal bread crumbs 114
  rhubarb brioche and butter
    pudding 116
  roasted and raw beet soup with
    rye bread 106–107
  Romesco sauce 112–13
  soups 102–109
  spaghetti with broccoli, chile, and
    sautéed bread crumbs 115
  Spanish chicken with a saffron
    and almond sauce 110
  summer panzanella 97
  summer pudding 120
  winter panzanella 98–99
brioche 92
  rhubarb brioche and butter
    pudding 116
brisket with pickled walnuts and
  celery root 58
broccoli
  grilled broccoli with Romesco
    112–13
  spaghetti with broccoli, chile, and
    fried bread crumbs 115
brown Betty
  baked peach 118
  blackberry and apple 156

brownies, chocolate 44
butter
  anchovy butter 139
  butter cookies 53
  sage butter 168

C
cabbage
  colcannon 57
  sausage and mustard casserole
    with cabbage and chestnuts 62
cakes
  almond cake with apricot jam 41
  banana blondies 46
  bay, honey, and lemon cake 50
  carrot cake with lime and
    mascarpone topping 36
  chocolate brownies 44
  chocolate cake 38
  date and coffee sponge cake 81
  dried apricot upside-down cake 40
  dried cranberry and cinnamon
    friands 49
  Earl Grey fruit tea loaf 43
  Eva's potato apple cake 24
  ham and Comté cake 90
  Parmesan potato cake 26
  rich chocolate truffle cake 78
calamari, stuffed 134
caramel
  caramel and cardamom ice cream
    with Tarocco oranges 151
  cardamom and orange crème
    caramel with nut brittle 82
cardamom
  caramel and cardamom ice cream
    with Tarocco oranges 151
  cardamom and orange crème
    caramel with nut brittle 82
carrots
  brisket with pickled walnuts and
    celery root 58
  carrot, apple, and blue cheese
    soup 131
  carrot cake with lime and
    mascarpone topping 36
  oxtail stewed with grapes 59
  tomato sauce with carrot, basil,
    and cream 174
casseroles see stews

celery root
  alternative cottage pie 19
  brisket with pickled walnuts and
    celery root 58
cheese
  baked beans with a green herb
    and Parmesan crust 180
  carrot, apple, and blue cheese
    soup 131
  chicken Savoyarde 15
  crushed peas with feta and
    scallions 124
  fried mozzarella sandwich 100
  ham and Comté cake 90
  Japanese squash gnocchi with
    sage butter 168
  leek and potato patty with blood
    sausage and cheese 179
  meatballs 21
  Parmesan potato cake with
    mozzarella and prosciutto 26–7
  pizza 184
  spicy chicken wings with blue
    cheese dressing 10
  tartiflette 89
  see also mascarpone
chestnuts
  chocolate and chestnut terrine
    76–77
  sausage and mustard casserole
    with cabbage and chestnuts 62
chickpeas 28–33
  chickpea and smoked paprika
    soup 30
  chickpea masala 166
  chorizo and chickpea stew with
    piquillo peppers 29
  falafel with tahini cream sauce 33
  hummus 28
  orange-scented lamb with
    chickpeas, rice, and yogurt 63
chicken 6–15
  braised chicken and rice with
    orange, saffron, almond, and
    pistachio syrup 140
  chicken savory cobbler with bell
    peppers and tomatoes 67
  chicken Savoyarde 15
  lemon chicken risotto 11
  poaching 14

roast chicken with sausage, sage,
    and prune stuffing 8–9
  Spanish chicken with a saffron
    and almond sauce 110
  spicy chicken wings with blue
    cheese dressing 10
  stock 14
chicken livers
  spiced chicken liver mousse with
    blackened onions 128
chiles
  aloo palak (spiced potato and
    spinach) 166
  falafel with tahini cream sauce
    33
  liver and onions with chile, lime,
    and fish sauce 144
  Romesco sauce 112–13
  spaghetti with broccoli, chile, and
    fried bread crumbs 115
  tomato chile jam 162
chocolate
  baked bitter chocolate custards
    79
  banana blondies 46
  bitter chocolate sorbet 84
  chocolate and chestnut terrine
    76–77
  chocolate brownies 44
  chocolate cake 38
  rich chocolate truffle cake 78
  white chocolate and raspberry
    truffles 74
chorizo and chickpea stew with
    piquillo peppers 29
chutney, mint 167
clafoutis
  fig and raspberry clafoutis 145
  prune clafoutis 145
clams
  paella with spring vegetables 170
coffee
  bitter chocolate sorbet 84
  chocolate brownies 44
  chocolate cake 38
  date and coffee sponge cake 81
  tiramisu 88
colcannon 57
cookies, butter 53
cottage pie 19

cranberries
  dried cranberry and cinnamon
    friands 49
cream
  Piedmont panna cotta 85
  see also ice cream
crème caramel, cardamom and
  orange 82
crème fraîche, pheasant braised with
  endive, white wine, and 68
croissants 92, 116
cucumber
  gazpacho 109
  salad Niçiose 176
  summer panzanella 97
  wild salmon with smoked
    eggplant polenta and hot
    cucumber 136–137
curries
  chickpea masala 166
custards
  baked bitter chocolate custards 79
  cardamom and orange crème
    caramel with nut brittle 82
  general satisfaction 86
  pea, mint, and scallop custards
    126–127
  rhubarb brioche and butter
    pudding 116
  summer berry gratin 148

D
dates
  date and coffee sponge cake 81
  whole-wheat date scones 47
  winter fruit salad 146
dressing, blue cheese 10
dried fruit
  dried cranberry and cinnamon
    friands 49
  Earl Grey fruit tea loaf 43
dumplings, mustard and thyme 57

E
Earl Grey fruit tea loaf 43
eggplant
  baked penne with eggplant and
    tomatoes 182
  wild salmon with smoked
    eggplant polenta 136–137

eggs
  Italian meat loaf 20–21
  racing eggs 101
  salade Niçoise 176
  Spanish tortilla 169
endive
  pheasant braised with endive,
    white wine, and crème fraîche
    68
  winter panzanella 98–99
Eva's potato apple cake 24

F
falafel with tahini cream sauce
  33
farls, potato 23
fennel
  little fish fillets with braised
    fennel and anchovy butter 139
feta, crushed peas with scallions and
  124
figs
  fig and raspberry clafoutis 145
  stuffed pork fillet with figs and
    Marsala 143
finnan haddie
  one-pot fish pie with spinach and
    leeks 69
fish
  bread crumbs to coat 114
  little fish fillets with braised fennel
    and anchovy butter 139
  one-pot fish pie with spinach and
    leeks 69
  see also mackerel, salmon, etc.
friands, dried cranberry and
  cinnamon 49
fruit 152–159
  baked peach brown Betty 118
  compote 119
  summer berry gratin 148
  summer pudding 120
  winter fruit salad 146
  see also apples, oranges, etc.

G
garlic
  pa amb oli, pa amb tomàquet
    96
  Provençal bread crumbs 114

gazpacho 109
general satisfaction 86
ginger
  rhubarb brioche and butter
    pudding 116
gnocchi, Japanese squash, with sage
  butter 168
grapefruit
  winter fruit salad 146
gratin, summer berry 148
green beans
  salade Niçoise 176
grilled broccoli with Romesco
  112–13
ground meat 16–21
  cottage pie 19
  Italian meat loaf 20–21
  meatballs stuffed with mozzarella
    21
  shepherd's pie 19

H
ham and Comté cake 90
hazelnuts
  nut brittle 82
  Romesco sauce 112–13
honey, bay, and lemon cake 50
hummus 28

I
ice cream, caramel and cardamom
  151
Italian meat loaf 20–21

J
jam
  general satisfaction 86
  tomato chile jam 162
Japanese squash gnocchi with sage
  butter 168

K
kidneys
  lamb and kidney pudding with a
    rosemary crust 64

L
ladyfingers
  general satisfaction 86
  tiramisu 88

lamb
  lamb and kidney pudding with a rosemary crust 64
  orange-scented lamb with chickpeas, rice, and yogurt 63
  shepherd's pie 19
lasagna, autumn vegetable 70
lavender butter cookies 53
leeks
  colcannon 57
  leek and potato patty with blood sausage and cheese 179
  one-pot fish pie with spinach and leeks 69
lemon
  bay, honey, and lemon cake 50
  lemon chicken risotto 11
  lemon curd 50
lime and mascarpone topping, carrot cake with 36
liver
  liver and onions with chile, lime, and fish sauce 144
  spiced chicken liver mousse with blackened onions 128

M
mackerel
  broiled mackerel with green and black olive salsa 173
  pickled mackerel and potato salad 130
mascarpone
  carrot cake with lime and mascarpone topping 36
  tiramisu 88
mashed potatoes 22–27
meat
  ground meat 16–21
  Italian meat loaf 20–21
  meatballs 21
  one-pot dinners 54–65
  see also beef, lamb, etc.
meringue
  general satisfaction 86
Middle Eastern stuffed peppers 132–33
mint chutney 167
mousse, spiced chicken liver 128
mozzarella sandwich, fried 100

mushrooms
  autumn vegetable lasagna 70
  mushroom soup with spices and bread 105
mussels
  paella with spring vegetables 170
mustard
  mustard and thyme dumplings 57
  sausage and mustard casserole with cabbage and chestnuts 62

N
navy beans
  baked beans with a green herb and Parmesan crust 180
nut brittle 82

O
olive oil
  pa amb oli, pa amb tomàquet 96
olives
  broiled sardines or mackerel with green and black olive salsa 173
  ham and Comté cake 90
  Italian meat loaf 20–21
  winter panzanella 98–99
one-pot dinners 54–71
one-pot fish pie with spinach and leeks 69
onions
  liver and onions with chile, lime, and fish sauce 144
  Spanish tortilla 169
  spiced chicken liver mousse with blackened onions 128
oranges
  braised chicken and rice with orange, saffron, almond, and pistachio syrup 140
  caramel and cardamom ice cream with Tarocco oranges 151
  cardamom and orange crème caramel with nut brittle 82
  orange-scented lamb with chickpeas, rice, and yogurt 63
  winter fruit salad 146
oven-dried tomatoes 161
oxtail stewed with grapes 59

P
pa amb oli, pa amb tomàquet 96
paella with spring vegetables 170
pain perdu with fruit compote 119
pan bagna 179
pancotto (bread soup) 104
panna cotta, Piedmont 85
panzanella 97–99
paprika
  chickpea and smoked paprika soup 30
Parmesan potato cake with mozzarella and prosciutto 26–27
pasta
  autumn vegetable lasagna 70
  baked penne with eggplant and tomatoes 182
  pasta con la Mollica 183
  spaghetti with broccoli, chile, and sautéed bread crumbs 115
peaches
  baked peach brown Betty 118
peas
  crushed peas with feta and scallions 124
  pea, mint, and scallop custards 126–7
penne with eggplant and tomatoes 182
peppers
  chicken or rabbit savory cobbler with bell peppers and tomatoes 67
  chorizo and chickpea stew with piquillo peppers 29
  gazpacho 109
  Middle Eastern stuffed peppers 132–33
  salade Niçoise 176
  Spanish tortilla 169
  winter panzanella 98–99
pheasant braised with endive, white wine, and crème fraîche 68
pickled mackerel and potato salad 130
pie crust 13
Piedmont panna cotta 85
pies
  cottage pie 19

one-pot fish pie with spinach and
leeks 69
sausage pie 12–13
shepherd's pie 19
piquillo peppers, chorizo and
chickpea stew with 29
pistachio nuts
braised chicken and rice with
orange, saffron, almond, and
pistachio syrup 140
nut brittle 82
pizza 184
plums, stewed 154–55
poaching chicken 14
polenta
wild salmon with smoked
eggplant polenta and hot
cucumber 136–37
pork
braised pork with quince 60
Italian meat loaf 20–21
pork and apple stuffing 13
stuffed pork fillet with figs and
Marsala 143
see also sausages
potatoes 22–27
aloo palak (spiced potato and
spinach) 166
colcannon 57
cottage pie 19
Eva's potato apple cake 24
leek and potato patty with blood
sausage and cheese 179
one-pot fish pie with spinach and
leeks 69
Parmesan potato cake with
mozzarella and prosciutto 26–7
pickled mackerel and potato salad
130
potato bread 23
shepherd's pie 19
Spanish tortilla 169
tartiflette 89
prosciutto, Parmesan potato cake
with mozzarella and 26–27
Provençal bread crumbs 114
prunes
prune clafoutis 145
roast chicken with sausage, sage,
and prune stuffing 8–9

Q
quail eggs 101
quince, braised pork with 60

R
rabbit savory cobbler with bell
peppers and tomatoes 67
racing eggs 101
raspberries
fig and raspberry clafoutis 145
summer berry gratin 148
summer pudding 120
white chocolate and raspberry
truffles 74
rhubarb
pain perdu with fruit compote
119
rhubarb brioche and butter
pudding 116
rice
braised chicken and rice with
orange, saffron, almond, and
pistachio syrup 140
lemon chicken risotto 11
Middle Eastern stuffed peppers
132–33
orange-scented lamb with
chickpeas, rice, and yogurt 63
paella with spring vegetables 170
stuffed calamari 134
risotto, lemon chicken 11
roasted and raw beet soup with rye
bread 106–7
Romesco sauce, grilled broccoli
with 112–13
roots, roasted 144
rosemary
butter cookies 53
lamb and kidney pudding with a
rosemary crust 64

S
sabayon
summer berry gratin 148
saffron
braised chicken and rice with
orange, saffron, almond, and
pistachio syrup 140
Spanish chicken with a saffron
and almond sauce 110

sage butter, Japanese squash
gnocchi with 168
salads
pickled mackerel and potato salad
130
salade Niçoise 176
summer panzanella 97
winter fruit salad 146
winter panzanella 98–99
salami
Parmesan potato cake with
mozzarella and prosciutto 26–27
salmon with smoked eggplant
polenta and hot cucumber
136–37
salsa, green and black olive 173
sandwiches
fried mozzarella sandwich 100
pan bagna 179
sardines, broiled, with green and
black olive salsa 173
sauces
Romesco 112–13
tahini cream sauce 33
tomato balsamico 174
tomato sauce with carrot, basil,
and cream 174
tomato sauce with pantry
additions 175
sausages
chicken or rabbit savory cobbler
with bell peppers and tomatoes
67
chorizo and chickpea stew with
piquillo peppers 29
pork and apple stuffing 13
racing eggs 101
roast chicken with sausage, sage,
and prune stuffing 8–9
sausage and mustard casserole
with cabbage and chestnuts 62
sausage pie 12–13
stuffed pork fillet with figs and
Marsala 143
savoy cabbage
colcannon 57
sausage and mustard casserole
with cabbage and chestnuts 62
scallions, crushed peas with feta and
124

scallops
    pea, mint, and scallop custards
      126–27
scones, whole-wheat date 47
shepherd's pie 19
single-pot dinners 54–71
slow-roasted whole tomatoes 161
smoked haddock
    one-pot fish pie with spinach and
      leeks 69
sorbets
    bitter chocolate sorbet 84
    blackberry sorbet 159
    black currant sorbet 159
soups 102–109
    carrot, apple, and blue cheese
      soup 131
    chickpea and smoked paprika
      soup 30
    gazpacho 109
    mushroom soup with spices and
      bread 105
    pancotto (bread soup) 104
    roasted and raw beet soup with
      rye 106–107
spaghetti
    pasta con la Mollica 183
    spaghetti with broccoli, chile, and
      sautéed bread crumbs 115
Spanish chicken with a saffron and
    almond sauce 110
Spanish tortilla 169
spiced chicken liver mousse with
    blackened onions 128
spicy chicken wings with blue
    cheese dressing 10
spinach
    aloo palak (spiced potato and
      spinach) 166
    one-pot fish pie with spinach and
      leeks 69
    Spanish tortilla 169
squash
    autumn vegetable lasagna 70
    Japanese squash gnocchi with
      sage butter 168
stewed plums 154–55
stews and casseroles
    beef stew with mustard and
      thyme dumplings 57

chorizo and chickpea stew with
    piquillo peppers 29
orange-scented lamb with
    chickpeas, rice, and yogurt 63
oxtail stewed with grapes 59
sausage and mustard casserole
    with cabbage and chestnuts 62
stock, chicken 14
strawberries
    pain perdu with fruit compote 119
    summer berry gratin 148
    summer pudding 120
stuffed
    bell peppers 132–33
    calamari 134
    pork fillet with figs and Marsala
      143
stuffings
    pork and apple stuffing 13
    sausage, sage, and prune stuffing
      8–9
sugar, vanilla 41
summer berry gratin 148
summer panzanella 97
summer pudding 120

T
tahini
    falafel with tahini cream sauce 33
    hummus 28
tarragon
    chicken Savoyarde 15
tartiflette 89
tea loaf, Earl Grey fruit 43
terrine, chocolate and chestnut
    76–77
tiramisu 88
tomatoes
    autumn vegetable lasagna 70
    baked penne with eggplant and
      tomatoes 182
    chicken or rabbit savory cobbler
      with bell peppers and tomatoes
      67
    gazpacho 109
    oven-dried tomatoes 161
    pa amb oli, pa amb tomàquet 96
    pizza 184
    Romesco sauce 112–13
    salade Niçoise 176

    slow-roasted whole tomatoes 161
    summer panzanella 97
    tomato balsamico 174
    tomato chile jam 162
    tomato sauce with carrot, basil,
      and cream 174
    tomato sauce with pantry
      additions 175
tortilla, Spanish 169
Treviso
    winter panzanella 98–99
truffles, white chocolate and
    raspberry 74
tuna
    salade Niçoise 176

V
vanilla sugar 41
veal
    Italian meat loaf 20–21
vegetables 166–170
    autumn vegetable lasagna 70
    paella with spring vegetables 170
    pizza 184
    roasted roots 144
    soups 102–109
    see also fennel, peppers, etc.

W
walnuts
    brisket with pickled walnuts and
      celery root 58
    carrot cake with lime and
      mascarpone topping 36
white chocolate and raspberry
    truffles 74
whole-wheat date scones 47
winter fruit salad 146
winter panzanella 98–99

Y
yogurt, orange-scented lamb with
    chickpeas, rice, and 63

Publishing director Jane O'Shea
Creative director Helen Lewis
Project editors Janet Illsley and
Eleanor Van Zandt
Art direction & design Lawrence Morton
Photographer James Merrell
Stylist Cynthia Inions
Editorial assistant Sarah Jones
Production director Vincent Smith
Production controller Aysun Hughes

First published in the United States
of America in 2010 by
Rizzoli International Publications,
Inc.
300 Park Avenue South
New York, NY 10010
www.rizzoliusa.com

Originally published in the United
Kingdom in 2009 by
Quadrille Publishing Limited
Alhambra House
27–31 Charing Cross Road
London WC2H 0LS
www.quadrille.co.uk

Text © 2009 Tamasin Day-Lewis
Photography © 2009 James Merrell
Design and layout © 2009 Quadrille
Publishing Limited

2010 2011 2012 2013 / 10 9 8 7 6 5 4 3 2 1

ISBN: 978-0-8478-3423-5

Library of Congress Control Number:
2009936370

Printed in China

For P. A lifetime of
friendship, music, and
good dinners is not to
be underestimated.
This book is for you,
in celebration of this
year's big event.

Praise for the *Supper for a Song* team:

Jane O'Shea for taking the idea and running with it
from start to finish

Janet Illsley for total attention to detail—no note too
small to escape her notice

Lawrence Morton, whose inspired art direction has
made it a book of beauty and wit

James Merrell, who has a painter's eye and has married
still life to composition, process to finished dish

Patricia Stone, a source of calm, fun, and occasional
hysteria—every kitchen needs all three—as she helped
cook the book for the photographs

Edward Latter, who helped cook on one of the shoots
and will surely go far

Alison Cathie, for inviting me to dance at Quadrille